The 2020 Vision
Of the
End Times

By
Trevor Maddison

Title: The 2020 Vision of the End Times

Edition: 1

Copyright © 2019 by Trevor Maddison

DEDICATION

I dedicate this book to the Great Multitude who are my family that are yet to be fully revealed.

Oh Gentle Lion
Oh Lamb That Roars

Oh My God, I Stand In AWE
My GOD, My GOD, I Need You MORE

Title: The 2020 Vision of the End Times
Genre: Religion, Christian, Eschatology
Author: Trevor Maddison
Date: 1st June 2019

Synopsis:
The history of mankind is approaching a key time…

In the middle months of 2020 there will be a WATERSHED moment that will bring a SEA CHANGE in the affairs of the world.

I am issuing this prophecy in mid-2019 as a right word for a right time. Things in the earth are about to change. I therefore find I am led to release this book as an explanation of that prophecy, as far as I have it, together with a fairly comprehensive statement of my understanding of the end times as God has given it to me over the years. I believe there are quite a number of key misconceptions out there that I am led to straighten out because an important time in God's plan is approaching. What I am sharing goes back as far as 1985 when God took me into a special season of discovery on this whole subject. Then these things seemed far off and I was restrained from writing about it, but now they seem imminent, which is probably why I now sense an urgency from God to write it down and pass it on. I haven't gone for a great deal of detail, but I've tried to focus on the things that really matter to you. For those that are scared by this whole subject let me urge you to take that fear to God because the Book of Revelation promises a real blessing to those that receive its message. Every God given promise in the scriptures holds true for you as a child of God if you have Jesus in your heart, even if the sea gets rough. What you need now is for God to fully and thoroughly prepare your heart and mind for those times to come.

TABLE OF CONTENTS

PREFACE

I grew up in a Christian home and I remember as a child of age five or less, the experience of God's presence in some of the special church events my parents took me to. This was something different to normal church which was mostly quite boring and arduous for me as a child. Had that been the limit of my experience I am not sure I would have retained anything, but this experience of the presence of God was powerful and despite my shy disposition I responded to the alter-call (a common practice then) to surrender my life to Christ. My parents didn't get what it took for me to do that as a shy child, and I don't think they took it seriously despite the fact they emphatically believed in salvation by this kind of surrender. I think they thought I was too young to understand and I was just following the crowd, maybe, but the presence of God is actually often something more discernible to children than it is to grown-ups with their inner battles and distractions. No, I was completely serious about it – as much as anything else I ever had been serious about up to that point. Later I rebelled against the religious churchy stuff and leaned more to my understanding, for which much of this faith thing didn't fit. But God didn't forget, and so he engineered the circumstances so that I came back to him the evening before my 18th birthday in response to a prayer I had prayed several years earlier asking him to make the truth of himself clear to me before the age of 18. And so I entered into a new phase of my Christian walk, which was to dive headlong into the religion, and then after a time to be led back out of that and realise what I have is a relationship which the religious elements tend to hinder rather than help.

That is my story in brief of how I became a Christian and what came after. I basically grew up in my faith. My spiritual growth was like my natural growth; I passed through a childhood and an adolescence. Along the way there were growth spurts as God led me the whole time. One of those came when I reached the seven year mark as a Christian (since age 18, now aged 25) and it took the form of God leading me into the End Times scriptures. This season lasted a few months, and then as quickly as I had been led into it, God led me out again and on to other things. I knew at that point to continue digging into End Times would not be the best thing for me; there were higher priorities waiting which were God's new direction for me. But that season was incredibly formative, and unforgettable. The only way I can describe it is it seemed to really sharpen me up. Of course all seasons with God mean growth, in some way, but this seemed special. When I came out of it I had an unshakeable conviction of two things – First that God has a plan. And second, that he has total control of this world and what will happen right up to the end, including the outcome of this age. As I came to the end of that season of learning I didn't have all the answers, and I still don't, but I discovered some definite keys. These I regard as the things God knows I really need to know – the things that relate mostly to the times I will actually live in. The rest I have more vague ideas about but not with the same conviction because it is the keys I have been given that will directly affect me, and many others like me who share them. Now I find myself approaching 35 years on from that experience, now aged 58, and suddenly I am led into it again. This time though, it is a bit different. I now have a sense of imminence to it all, whereas back then it seemed far off. I knew back then it all had a purpose. Now I feel that its purpose is about to begin to be realised.

That sense of imminence I have led to the prophecy that is the basis of this book and it gave me my sense of urgency to write about it – something I believe is God given. That prophecy focuses on events that I believe will take place in 2020, which at the time of writing is next year, and which also explains why I feel this is the right time for it.

The instant reaction of many people to End Times teaching (eschatology as some call it) is to bury our heads in the sand like the proverbial ostrich we have all heard about. I partially understand that. After all, there are some scary things in it, and none of us like to be scared do we – or at least we don't like it when we realise it may be real and not just something fictional that can be contained in an image box like the ones we watch quite a lot these days. But that reticence to face these things is something that can change very quickly at the point where it actually arrives in our reality and proves true. If the monsters we watch came out of our TV I'm guessing we would clear the room pretty quickly. If that happens with prophecy then suddenly, for many, not knowing becomes scarier than knowing, so we are forced to seek answers as we scrabble to find a sense of security again. It is in anticipation of that reaction that I am writing this down, and because for the most part before it happens I pretty much expect the message to be ignored even though I have done what I can to put it out there. After all, I understand that there is a huge amount written on the topic of End Times, which is another reason why people ignore it – there is just not the time to sort out what is true from what is false, especially given that in the end it could all turn out to have been a waste of time because all of it was wrong. However, in the case of this book there is a clear prediction about something coming in 2020 that seems likely it will rock our world and maybe our faith if it happens. That prophecy comes together with the timing of that event, so that must speak for itself. Otherwise if it doesn't happen you can confidently discard this book and I will acknowledge the error and make sure I don't ever make the same mistake again. That said, I still wouldn't advise anyone to put this on the back burner and do nothing with it other than wait to see if it pans out. If you are a Christian you can take this to God for yourself and get your own conviction about it, as I have. That is how we are supposed to live and it will make sure you are prepared if and when this proves to be correct as I currently sincerely believe it will.

Having cleared all that up, let me say the approach I have taken is to try to pass on to you almost the whole of my knowledge on this subject, though not just to dump it all on you which may be a bit overwhelming, but to do it in a prioritised way so you best understand the things that will most affect you first and the most, and the things that are a lower priority I cover later but give less emphasis to. I guess if events progress and this pans out then in time those later things will become your priority, and so I have also written with a view to informing you who get to those things in their time in order to help you as much as I can when you need it.

One thing I believe about Bible prophecy as a whole is that much of it has meaning that has not yet been revealed. When I look at the Minor Prophets for example, some things seem crystal clear, and others are totally obscure. Often these things are found side by side. At times the New Testament puts its finger on an Old Testament prophecy that marks it out to mean something definite. They are useful markers that help us interpret the rest, but still there is a whole lot where we seem to be left guessing. Or a least we seem to be for now. I believe even if we don't have a handle on it, God does. Our understanding of it depends emphatically on him. Actually this is true of all scripture but I think when it comes to other matters, such as things to do with life, we feel more familiar and therefore more able to interpret it on our own, which is a mistake. Think about it. If the scriptures are really sourced in God, which most of the church seems pretty certain about, then it came from an omniscient mind – a mind of infinite knowledge, wisdom and understanding. Therefore we surely should expect it to have a depth that is hard to fully fathom for a peanut like ours. Ok, that omniscient mind has decided to speak to us personally through it so we should expect to be able to understand it in some measure, but we shouldn't be surprised if it goes deeper than we do. When it comes to End Times prophecy that depth becomes more obvious than ever. In truth what we have from God is the revelation of it that he chooses to give us for our time, but the rest of it only unfolds as and when it is needed, and as God chooses to give it. Therefore, as I wrote earlier, we can expect the things that we are going to live through to be much clearer than those things that are further off, or that do not belong to our era. We expect those things will be revealed more fully when the time approaches to those people that will actually live through it. We of course have an interest and a fascination in those things, and God has not left us completely unsatisfied there, but we have to accept there is a level of mystery to it all, and in fact we should be really happy about that. In the end our real comfort is not in knowing it all, but in simply knowing that God knows.

All that amounts to my disclaimer on being clearer about some of the End Times scriptures than others. I will focus on what I think is of key importance to us. For the rest I will pass comment on things I believe and I will make a few declared speculations, but I will also be clear that for those things I am more uncertain of their full meanings. I hope you can accept this – it is just how things are, and are supposed to be.

One thing you may have realised is I originally wrote this largely for Christians as I expected them to be the audience for the message. But having completed the work I realised this is an important message for all people, and probably even more so for those who have no faith, or for those that are from a different belief. If that is you then you may be interested, before you proceed, to read the appendix I added towards the end specifically to help you get started (Appendix 1). It will explain the things you really, really need to know, not just to understand the book better, but about life and the realities that exist behind what is seen in this physical world which is where all this came from. Sometimes we Christians are so familiar with dealing in those things we forget not everybody has that experience, so our language and jargon develops to create a bit of a gap between believers and sceptics. It you read that section it will not only inform you, but it has potential to lead you to the very source of the things I am about to share with you, which means you can find much more 'revelation' on this and many other things for yourself.

1. The 2020 Prophecy

Let's cut the chase. The prophecy I have for you is this:

In the middle months of 2020 there will be a WATERSHED moment that will bring a SEA CHANGE in the affairs of the world.

The first thing to say is, this is the prophecy I have in its purest form. In many ways that is the headline version, but I also want to offer some explanation of what I believe it means, and give you the history of how and when I received it. Jesus did a similar thing when he spoke in parables but then later explained the meaning. That was often to conceal it from some and reveal it to others, but in this case it is more about me getting the basic message across so you before trying to give you any details that could swamp you with words rather than clarify the matter. In this case an explanation of terms is warranted because there are some metaphors in it that need explanation.

WATERSHED means – an event or period marking a turning point in a situation.

SEA CHANGE means – a profound or notable transformation.

Middle Months – I believe this means in the middle six months, and probably in the middle four months of the year 2020, though this is a derived date as I will explain soon.

First of all let me say this prophetic word itself as a whole was received, not derived, so my claim is those words are not my own and I am just the messenger. They may therefore have further meaning that I am not yet aware of.

So please note that by contrast the explanations that follow are partly of my derivation, but I still believe them so I feel I should offer those things to you with this disclaimer – this is what I think it all means. What I am saying is it is quite possible the word itself may prove correct, but the explanation may prove to be wrong, and we have to allow for that. For example, later I will share a possible meaning of the word 'watershed' that didn't initially occur to me when I first received the prophetic word, but there is a strong case for it so it may well be true, therefore I am going to share it, though I will usually warn you if it is a speculation. Of course there are more elements of this that are quite certain for me because they also seemed to come to me more like direct revelations, rather than through study or derivation, so I will try to pass on my sense of my personal certainty about things as I discuss them. This is how it always is for the whole of the prophetic. The reason is because God does not allow us to operate alone, or to rely entirely on someone else. We have to include him in the process, so each of you needs God to reveal things directly to you for it to be of any benefit to you. My words are only the fuel for that, but God within you is the fire that consumes it all.

The symbolic word 'sea' has a definite meaning in the book of Revelation, but it may have other meanings too that are relevant. It symbolises the masses of people. A sea can therefore be like the sea of glass, or crystal, symbolising a multitude of people in a place of peace or rest, or it can be roaring and foaming symbolising a multitude of people in a place of activity or unrest. I believe what this is saying is there will be a change in the world that happens at a very specific point – the watershed – where the multitude of people move from one state to another like a sea state changing from one weather state to another.

Thirdly, let's look at the timing I have given which is the middle months of 2020, and my explanation that it means the middle 6 months of 2020, and most probably the middle 4 months of the year.

Why am I not certain about that? The reason is the timing of it is derived, as I said earlier, so I need to show you how I derived it and why I cannot give you a definite date. Of course if God wanted to give us a definite date he could, but this implies that he doesn't. He just wants us to be ready and to have an idea of the season, which is not the only time he has done that. However, if you have a hotline to God and can get more info on this I would be more than happy to hear about it. Now let me tell you how I derived this timing.

Sometime in the year 2020 the total world population reaches a significant number. That number is 7,777,777,777 people, and that I believe is the 'watershed' number. So I am saying this 'sea change' will happen at the point the population hits that number. However we don't know exactly when that is. We only know the ballpark, so it could occur anywhere in the time window I have given. That is something I have calculated from the best figures I can obtain for it. The timing part of the prophecy is therefore derived but it is tied to this key population number.

Why this number? Well, this number is 10x7s. Ten is the number of man with our ten digits, and the decimal number system we all use that was derived from that. It also signifies completion because when we reach ten we increment the next order of our decimal number. Then the number 7 is the number of God, and of perfection, as often seen in the Bible – e.g. the seven spirits of God. So 10x7s represents God's point of perfect completion where the number of man meets the number of God.

This may seem weird but it is not the only timeclock we know of in scripture of this kind that God is keeping or telling us about. You won't find the 10x7s number in the Bible so this is something I am claiming to be a revealed truth specifically for this time, though God often declines to give us exact dates but he does sometimes give us concepts like this.

The other timeclock of this sort I mentioned is very clearly given to us from scripture as the one that marks the very end of this age; the end of the age of tribulation – or trouble; before there is a transition to the time of wrath. I will explain all this later, but this end-of-the-age timeclock is in fact the number of people that have been martyred for their faith in Christ. In the breaking of the fifth seal in Rev 7:11 we see these martyred souls under the alter asking God when the end will come and their blood will be avenged – i.e. when will the day of wrath or punishment come – and they are told to wait a little longer until the full number of their brethren who are to be martyred have come in. So although the actual number of martyrs is not revealed to us, and it may not help us if it were, nevertheless the timing of the end of the age is keyed directly to the count of the martyrs that have come in and the end of the age will come when it reaches that 'full number'. It is therefore perfectly consistent that God also has some kind of timeclock on the beginning of the troubles that mark the end of the age and I will explain that further in just a moment. What I am saying, or rather prophesying, is that the beginning of the end is tied to the total population with the 10x7s number in the same way that the end of the age is timed by the number of martyrs. In our day there are 100,000+ martyrs per year so this figure is constantly rising. That means on average more than 250 people per day are martyred for their faith, even on this day! In the past this annual number has been higher – even 3 times higher, so the clock on the end of the age is ticking all the time.

Why should God give us a timer on the beginning of the end of the age troubles rather than just on the end itself? Good question. I am glad you asked. The reason is the scripture represents this age as a pregnancy where at the end of the age there is a birthing (Rom 8: 19 & 22). The creation is described as standing on tiptoe waiting for this birthing to take place when the 'sons of God will be revealed'. That means the birthing of all of us together that have been born again and have Christ within; the body of Christ – these are the sons of God. As we know with a normal pregnancy there is a definite beginning to that final birthing process which is the time when the birth pains begin. This is the time I am prophetically saying is marked by God's with the 10x7s timeclock, and that number I have calculated from current data will be reached in the middle months of 2020.

At this point I need to branch off a little into other contemporary prophecies that have been given by men that have been recognised and accepted by many to have revelations of God for our times. Remember Joel prophesied that the last days would be marked by people who prophesy, have visions, and see dreams (Joel 2:28) – in fact that all of us would have these things, or they would be available. Peter confirmed that these are the days of those things when the baptism of the Spirit first fell and he quoted that Joel scripture (Act 2:17-18). The prophetic voice I am calling in here is a man called *Bob Jones* who graduated (i.e. died) in 2014. He prophesied many things and saw many fulfilments of his words, but probably the most significant prophecy he gave us he called a '100 year prophecy' that covered God's purposes in each decade from the 1950s through to the 2050s. I refer to this because I resonate with this as much as anything I have received myself, and its message has served to fill some gaps in my understanding about where we are in this age, at this time, and what to expect up to the end. Also, it does seem right to me that the prompt to emphasize his words should come just 5 years after his death. I have observed that the fulfilment of the words of some prophets are often triggered on their death, or shortly after.

One great thing is that Bob's prophecy on this is not at all apocalyptic in nature, but is entirely positive, which I think will be a relief to some of us. That I believe is because it is the view of the advancement of the Kingdom of God in these times. After all a birthing is a scary thing but it is also a time that leads to immense joy and blessing. Whilst the world is passing through trouble, the church is continuing to grow and advance towards the completion where the birthing will finally reveal it for what it is. To see the complete picture Bob's prophecy has to be aligned with scripture so we understand how those things relate and fit together.

https://www.youtube.com/watch?v=qZJzwnyLod0

You can see this message directly for yourself delivered by Bob on YouTube, but let's take a look at what he said. For each decade Bob highlighted the major advancement of the Kingdom of God that would take place. First let me simply mention the decades that are now past – 1950: The POWER of God; 1960s – The SPIRIT of God; 1970s: the WORD of God; 1980s: The PROPHETS of God; 1990s:

The GOVERNMANT of God; 2000s: The GLORY of God; 2010s: The FAITH of God.

For myself I recognise how these things have already happened, and that for each decade the aspect of the Kingdom discovered there has persisted to this day. That brings us to what Bob said about what is to come. Let's focus on this a little more closely:

2020s – The REST of God
2030s – The FAMILY of God
2040s – The KINGDOM of God
2050s – The SONS of God

I strongly encourage you to listen to Bob Jones directly on this because he adds details that fill some of the gaps and help us to understand what is meant by these words.

My first point is, though I note Bob didn't say it directly in the YouTube clip I refer to, this appears to be a prophecy up to the End Time – the end of the age. The reason I say this is because it culminates in a decade that reveals the very thing that Paul tells us marks the end of this age, which he describes as a birthing process at the end of which the 'sons of God will be revealed' – i.e. birthed (Rom 8: 19 & 22). Paul also says that the creation has been groaning in the pains of child birth right up to the present time as it approaches this moment of birth.

What I am suggesting as an interpretation of the prophecy I have given, together with Paul's prophecy in Romans and that of Bob Jones, is this: The whole of this development of the body of Christ is a pregnancy – one that I might point out has taken much longer than the Apostle Paul thought it ever would because that timing of the end was not revealed to him. Nor was it, or is it revealed to Jesus, or the Holy Spirit it seems, but only the Father knows – incredibly! However Jesus did say to us we would know the time has arrived by the signs we see that correlate to the things he prophesied would come in the world. Much has been written on all of that – including incredible things like the return of Israel as a nation after nearly 2000 years, but also martyrdom and persecution. The point I was getting at here is that a pregnancy has a definite ending with a birthing, and a definite start to that ending of the pregnancy when the actual birth pains begin.

As most women that have been through pregnancy can tell you, pregnancy has its troubles all the way along. But the major trauma of that whole process most definitely comes at the end when the child is actually born. For a first birth that process normally takes on average about 8 hours. My explanation of the prophetic word I am bringing is that it marks that beginning of the end when the real pain and trauma starts. What seems really appropriate about this is that Bob's prophecy puts us just 40 years or so from that end where the birthing is complete and the 'sons of God are revealed' – i.e. born. For those of us that know our Bibles we will straight away recognise that 40 is a significant number in the Bible, often related to a final period before a change in epoch. I will leave that study to you, but it's worth doing. Does Bob Jones therefore claim to know the time of the end? – not exactly, but it does bring us within the season we expect it to happen, given the present signs to confirm it; though we must be aware there are warnings that when it does come there will be something unexpected about the timing, and it will be sudden. That I believe is simply because though the Spirit within us gives us a witness about many things – even all things – the one exception is the actual time of the end. We simply have no God given information on that for the simple reason the Holy Spirit doesn't even know it. For that reason you can confidently discard predictions by people who place it a long time, or even hundreds of years ahead. They simply cannot know this and if they did it would defeat part of God's purpose in withholding that information from us – to keep us alert. The other part may well be to keep the enemy guessing. That means there is still scope in all this for surprises, but there we are talking about the actual birthing at the End of the Age, whereas the prophecy I am bringing relates to the beginning of the birth pains of the last period up to the end which I am suggesting is in the year 2020 – the beginning of the final forty years – the beginning of birth pains.

I did mention something that didn't originally occur to me about the 'watershed' word when I first received it, even though it is an obvious thing. Watershed is exactly what happens when a birthing begins. It is often the first event at the beginning of contractions, or it comes soon after the contractions starts. That word may therefore have a direct meaning rather than just the metaphorical one I quoted – as the start of the process of creation birthing the sons of God, as the Apostle Paul wrote (Rom 8:19 & 22).

As an aside, if we take this analogy a little bit further and look at the whole period since the death of Christ as the beginning of pregnancy to the 2050s as the end of it; the last forty years equates proportionally to about the last 5 days before the birth. It is therefore getting well within range of a normal birthing.

One other thing that convinces me we are near the end is the very size of the world population. We are now down to an average land area per person of about 82m x 82m, or if we only count the habitable areas it's down to 70m x 70m each. Of course we actually bunch together in places more than that so there is more room and it is not a perfect view, but what it does tell us is we have covered the globe and this world is getting quite full so its resources are becoming quite stretched. For that reason alone I expect God to intervene to wrap it up before too long.

Now let me give you my history with this word, including the things I will be sharing in the rest of the book. I mentioned earlier that God took me into a season of End Times study and revelation in 1985 when I was just seven years old as a Christian. That particularly covered the breaking of the seals in Rev 6, the prophecies of Jesus, particularly in Matt 24, Mark 13 and Luke 21, various key chapters of the Book of Daniel, and parts of Zechariah that seem to align to some degree with the book of Revelation. I mentioned that after a few months in that period of 1985 I was led to move on, but I had a deep sense this knowledge and understanding had a purpose though the time for it seemed far off back then.

Leaping forward now to about a decade ago, around 2010, a lot of water went under the bridge since 1985; a whole lot spiritual growth, and a whole lot of experience of the power of the Spirit in various ways in the interim. Then, on this subject, when the world population was about to pass the 7 billion mark I was asking God if it had any significance given that 7 in a significant Bible number. I got no convictions about that number, but I did receive something pointing to the population number 7,777,777,777. I have therefore hung onto this word having done nothing more than calculate roughly when it would come (that's the geek God put in me). I shared it only very rarely as most of the time it didn't feel right to share it and I never really felt led to focus on it. At that time I didn't really have many details about its purpose. I guess in my own mind I speculated it may be the time of the end. In recent months what I found is this whole topic of the End of the Age rising in my Spirit in my personal times with God as I felt he was pointing me towards it again, possibly prompted by an awareness that the population was approaching this number and it was time to look into it again. Many times I have thought of writing what I learned about the Book of Daniel back in 1985 as no-one even now seems to have come to that revelation; not even on the internet. The other key revelation for me came from the Book of Revelation – particularly Rev 6 & 7, on the breaking of the seals, and the key truth was that there are actually two seasons there. One is the period of tribulation, and the other is the time of God's wrath. I will focus on this next, but this is a very important and key revelation for understanding the whole Book of Revelation. The transition from one time to the other is on the breaking of the 6th seal when we are explicitly told the day of the wrath of the Lamb has come (Rev 6:17). All that comes before this point is tribulation (i.e. trouble) and I relate that exactly to the birthing process. As I said, we will discuss this next.

2. Tribulation or Wrath

We now come to study the scriptures that define the time of tribulation – the time I am suggesting is the full pregnancy that in the end reveals the sons of God as the apostle Paul prophesied (Rom 8:19 & 22).

First of all let me restate something. Much of the teaching I have seen on the tribulation has been based on a definition of 'tribulation' that includes all the traumatic events on earth described in the Book of Revelation together. This includes the breaking of the seals in Rev 6 & 7, the seven trumpets and bowls of wrath that are poured out once all seals are broken, and the seven plagues that come last. This I believe is a major error. The truth is, there is a transition on this timeline that occurs on the breaking of the 6th seal where the world moves from the time of tribulation to the time of the wrath of the Lamb (Rev 6:16-17 esp. v17), and these times are very different in nature, as I will explain.

Tribulation simply means 'trouble' – it is not judgement or wrath; that is something else. Wrath is judgement – the vengeance of God poured out on his enemies. Paul makes clear in two separate statements that it is impossible for wrath to be poured out on his people – the church; the body of Christ (1 Thes 5:9, 1 Thes 1:10). This categorically tells us we, the people of God, are not appointed to suffer wrath. How could we be when Jesus has already taken that punishment for us and we are forgiven? For us to be here when God pours out his wrath is like pouring judgement on those who are already judged. In this chapter it is actually the Lamb of God – Jesus – that is unleashing these judgments when he finally breaks the last seal because God has entrusted ALL judgement to the Son (John 5:22). So did he suffer to then turn on us to pour out God's anger on us? – NO WAY! He has taken it for us. The judgement on earth is for all of God's enemies, and on this matter I believe there are some surprising truths because that does not just mean the remainder of the people left on earth that have not accepted him, as some think. There is more to it than that. However, though we are not appointed to suffer wrath, Jesus told us explicitly we will have trouble – i.e. tribulation (John 16:33), but we should take heart because he has overcome the world, and that too he has done for us – *he has overcome the tribulation for us*!

The difference between these two times is wide. The period of tribulation includes all that comes before the breaking of the 6th seal. Then the sixth seal wraps the tribulation period up so all is ready for the beginning of judgement as the last seal – the 7th seal, is opened. Everything in these first five seal are things we are already very familiar with on earth and they correlate very closely to the things Jesus warned us would come while we are still here. These tribulations include: war, murder, conquest, disease, pestilence, famine, natural disasters, death by wild animals, man-made disasters, desolations, persecution, martyrdom, false messiahs, false prophets, rampant sin. Does any of this sound familiar? We already live in days where all this kind of thing happens and it has done for a long time – ever since Jesus spoke about them and much of it before that. He said these things will continue to the end.

By contrast the judgements in the time of wrath that begin when the 7th seal is broken are a whole different ball game – they bring a whole different level of terror. They include the sounding of the seven trumpets and then the pouring out of bowls of wrath, followed by seven plagues on the earth. Now these judgements for a large part take on much more symbolic language and they describe events that are more horrific than anything seen in the breaking of the seals; the tribulation. There are things that in some ways resemble the tribulation but are on a whole new scale where seas are tuning to blood; stars are thrown down called 'Bitterness'; locusts appear with a sting in their tail; massive armies marching out with fire smoke and sulphur; there are darkness and demonic spirits mentioned. Suddenly all these images and symbols are really unfamiliar to the physical world we live in now – they are things we can't fully define. The basic reason for this is there is a whole spiritual dimensions to what is going on in the earth at this time, and this is wrath and judgement. I will explain this further but the point I am making right now is that this is not tribulation – i.e. trouble – it is the wrath of God, which means judgement, anger and vengeance of God.

We may ask why the time of wrath is reserved for one generation at the end when many evil people have come and gone, and there were many that went their own way in life and didn't seek or follow God. We ask, are this last generation so much worse than the rest to deserve it?

One reason is that a large proportion of all the people that ever lived will in fact be alive then, so they are not just a minority, but that is not all. Of course all people will be judged by God, but this time of wrath on earth is not just about the judgement of that generation of people on earth at that time. It is the judgement of the principalities and powers that until this time have been occupying the heavenly realms in all generations causing evil, but have now been forced down to the earth to be judged with them. In fact we may realise that the judgement of those principalities and powers is the main issue in that time, rather than the judgement of the people, though of course both are important in God's plan. What I am saying is that the time of wrath has become a spiritual thing and not just a natural thing as we know it, which explains the change in language and our unfamiliarity with the kind of judgements predicted. Joel also prophesies extensively about locusts as Revelation does and describes them with stings in their tails (Rev 9). These images are emphatically pointing to spiritual forces – demons and powers. The things that happen in tribulation, as bad as they are, are all things we have seen in some measure on the earth already. But the things that happen in the time of wrath after the transition are also largely spiritual in nature and that is what makes them so much more terrifying.

3. Rapture

A very good question has been asked which is: Where does the rapture (as we call it) happen in the Book of Revelation? The main scripture covering the events of the rapture at the return of Christ, where he gathers all that belong to him to himself, are found in 1 Thes 4:13-5:11, but locating them in the book of Revelation can be more of a challenge.

The word 'rapture' is not actually a Bible word. The Apostle Paul never really had a single word for it, he just described what would happen. The same goes for John in the Book of Revelation, which makes it a little more difficult to pinpoint there, but it's not really that hard to find. Rapture has become the common word that most Christians understand, but other words have been used. One is the 'evacuation' – which has the advantage that it is a commonly used word with a meaning, so it does what it says on the tin/can. But rapture is still a good word because this event is so unique it does deserve a special word to define it and help us refer to it.

In Rev 14:14-20, which comes after many of the scriptures I referred to describing the time of wrath, there is a harvest of some kind which has two parts. First the Son of Man gathers his harvest. Then an angel gathers someone who are left like grapes to be loading into the winepress of God's wrath. Again with these we see wrath exacted on some who for reasons already given cannot be the people of God. But is the first part of this harvest the rapture of the people of God? There are actually some that do teach a doctrine of the wicked being harvested and the church left to rule the earth – something that I think has just a kernel of truth in it which we will come to cover later, but to look at this as the rapture is a little confused because of the failure to recognise the difference between the time of tribulation and the time of wrath. For now let's continue to complete my understanding of the events before we consider that and we will see it all comes to fall into place.

What I will suggest to you is that this Rev 14 harvest is not the rapture but the winding up of the time of wrath, so all these events happen on earth. The rapture Paul wrote about did in fact happen earlier, right at the point of transition from the time of tribulation to the time of wrath. That transition occurs, as I have said before, on the breaking of the 6th seal. Where is that rapture in the Bible text of Revelation? The way it is expressed is in the very next chapter (Rev 7), before the breaking of the 7th seal – so judgement hasn't yet started, where we see the great multitude of every nation, tribe, people and language, standing in front of the throne of the Lamb, wearing white robes, waving palm branches, and shouting with a great roar – *"Salvation comes from our God who sits on the throne and from the Lamb"*. These are the 'saved' and now 'raptured' people of God, perfectly placed in the sequence of events on the breaking of the sixth seal.

Remember the chapter endings in the scriptures are a man-made construct that were not in the original text so the events of the sixth seal don't stop at the end of Rev 6, they carry on up to the breaking of the 7th seal, all still in chronological sequence but now showing events in heaven as well as on earth. Meeting chapter 7 in the middle of the 6th seal can suggest the events of the 6th seal end there and we are moving into the seal (7th), but that is just a consequence of the chapter numbers clashing with the text. In fact the whole of Rev 7 is still on the 6th seal and the 7th seal is not broken until the beginning of chapter 8.

So, on the breaking of the 6th seal we see 144,000 people 'sealed', meaning marked for a special purpose, and these appear to be back on earth. They are a special group of people who still have a job to do on earth in the time of wrath, but we will come to them later. First we have more to say about this raptured multitude of people we see next in Rev 7 because that is the vast majority of us who are the people of God.

Before we carry on with this, just to clear up one thing in case it is a problem – This 144,000 are not the whole body of Christ as some have suggested. That number is far too small. Abraham was promised a nation of descendants who Paul says in Romans have the same faith as he does, and as God promised they will number more than the sands of the seashores and the stars in the heavens – meaning they cannot be counted. This great multitude are called exactly that because, as it says, they too are too numerous to be counted (Rev 7:9). There is no question that this is the church, the people of God – US! Here in Rev 7, still on the breaking of the 6th seal, they have just been raptured from the earth and from the grave, and now appear before the throne in heaven where they are in an ecstatic state of praise at what God has done as they begin to shout declaring "*Salvation comes from God who sits on the throne and from the Lamb*". They know they have been saved from the wrath of the Lamb which is about to be poured out on the earth, but which the Lamb has already taken himself for those that have received him – the people now gathered before the throne. This is the place to be on that day, so whatever you do don't miss that party – trust me!

Just to clear up another thing now we have highlighted the difference between the time of tribulation and the time of the wrath of the Lamb, and located the rapture at the transition between the two – It becomes clear why the language often used to define different End Times ideas falls short of the mark. The *Pre-Tribulation* and *Post-Tribulation* ideas become particularly misleading where they attempt to locate the rapture either before or after tribulation as they define it. That is because the big problem here is their definition of the term tribulation as both the actual tribulation period (the seals) and the time of wrath combined. What I am showing is that the rapture actually takes place somewhere in the middle at the point of transition from one time to the next – from tribulation to wrath, so these ideas and terms fail to even allow for that possibility. What happens before that point of transition is tribulation. What happens after it is wrath, and these two are significantly different in many ways. If we want a term to properly define where the rapture happens as I am explaining it then it would be the rapture occurring *Post-Tribulation/Pre-Wrath* providing of course we are using the correct definition of the term tribulation.

Enough of the definition of terms for now. Let's reiterate what happens when the sixth seal is broken. First the saints, the people of God, are gathered in the rapture and appear before the throne of God in heaven as the great multitude from every nation, tribe, people and language. Secondly there is a natural cataclysmic earthquake event on earth and the people remaining there, who are not the people of God, that realise this is the long foretold day of judgement – i.e. the day of the wrath of the Lamb. Finally the 144,000 are sealed for their special purpose back on earth in the time of wrath and that concludes the preparation for the breaking of the 7th seal of the scroll, which is the final seal, so the scroll will then finally open and the judgement of God's wrath on earth can commence.

One point that should be made before we move on is about the worthiness of the Lamb to open this scroll. We see John weeping bitterly because no-one was found worthy to open the scroll. He is moved by the Spirit here feeling the heart and sentiment of heaven towards the earth. They are holy beings and they long for a holy outcome to this age with this world. They rejoice over salvation when it happens, but for those who will not repent they know their time must be limited. They know the scroll contains essential judgement because such a world cannot be tolerated indefinitely and the very thought of that as an eternal entity would be a torment to every holy creature of heaven, as sin was a torment to the soul of righteous Lot when he lived among the people of Sodom and Gomorrah. Then the Lamb of God steps forward. Only he is seen to be worthy because the opening of this scroll of judgement must also be a holy act so the person who opens it must be proved to be both holy and to be one who only ever acts in Love – for the highest good of all things. Christ proved his love on the cross by sacrificing himself and doing the utmost that could be done to redeem sinful man. Now having done that he is the one who is worthy to open this scroll of judgment and there is no room for any to ever accuse him of an act of tyranny or of lacking love for those that are judged by it having already submitted to suffer in such an extreme way himself before he unleashes such suffering upon others.

Still on the subject of 'rapture', the events in Revelation continue to progress chronologically into the time of wrath beginning with Rev 8 and the Trumpets, through to the end of Rev 10 at which point the angel says to John that he must prophesy again about many peoples, nations languages and kings. This tells us some of what follows goes over the same ground again so we see the same events that have already been covered from a different perspective. Even after this statement the chronological events continue up to the 7th and final trumpet taking us to the end of Rev 11, but then Rev 12 appears to take us back to cover some of the same ground again, this time giving us a heavenly perspective of the events already covered as we saw in Rev 7 after the breaking of the 6th seal.

In Rev 12 we see a pregnant woman in labour giving birth to a male child who will rule with a rod of iron. This we know from other scriptures is Jesus and it refers to a rule on earth that is yet to be established. What we also know from Paul's writings is that part of our destiny is to rule with Christ. We have a role to play in God's eternal plan where we rule with him. In fact as we will see, all the events that come on earth after rapture involve us in some way. Then in Rev 12 we see a red dragon standing over the woman waiting for the birth so he can devour the child. This dragon is clearly identified as the devil or Satan. At this point he occupies a place in the heavens, which aligns with Paul's statement that we wrestle not with flesh and blood but with principalities and powers in the heavenly realm. At the birth, before the dragon can devour the child it is snatched away. Here again is a reference to the rapture occurring right at the point of one of those cliff-hanger moments we see at every level from our personal life as God meets our needs at the last minute, right up to the global level in the events of the world. So the child is raptured. That leaves the mother. But also no sooner has the child been snatched away from harm on earth than there is war in heaven against the dragon and he is cast down to the earth having lost his place in heaven. This is an extremely important point. When rapture occurs we, the people of God, are caught up into the heavenlies and the throne of God, but at the same time Satan and his realm are cast down, losing his place in the heavenlies, so there is an exchange, and this is a complete reordering of the whole earthly and heavenly realm from the spiritual perspective.

The implications of all of this is radical. To understand it we should first realise that Satan has long since tried to occupy the earth along with keeping his place in the heavens, but has been prevented from doing so by the prayers, intercessions and deliverance ministry of the church on earth, accompanied by the work of powerful angels. In Thes 2:7 where Paul speaks of all these events we are told that something or someone holds back the Antichrist from emerging on earth until he is 'taken', or as may be more accurately translated he 'disappears from the midst'. The thing that holds back Antichrist on earth is Christ, and that means us in whom Christ dwells. He, Christ, is the only one strong enough to do this. The scripture Zech 5:5-11 I believe has a strong alignment to this which is important, especially given Zech 6:1-8 also has a strong alignment to Rev 6 and the breaking of the seals as I will explain later. In Zech 5 we see a woman called wickedness pushed down in a basket, then the basket is lifted by angels so it is suspended in the air (the heavens) until at the right time it is set in place on the earth in 'land of Babylonia'. This whole image is a picture of the position of Satan and his realm suspended in the heavenlies but not free to occupy the earth until he is permitted to do so.

I remember reading a very influential book in my early years as a Christian called *The Great Intercessor* about a man named *Rees Howells*. This guy was a remarkable person in many ways. Both in the way he lived his life on the ground dealing with the homeless, but also in his calling to be an intercessor. He lived in the times of the great wars, WW1 and WW2, which made his comments about those events particularly insightful and interesting.

One thing he said was '*Stalin is his own man, but Hitler could tell you the very day the spirit entered him*'. Another that I particularly want to highlight was an explanation from the whole of WW2. He said God called him to pray and intercede because *Satan was trying to force the end times ahead of its proper time.* I guess that's a bit like a general getting impatient for a pending battle and feeling like time spent in inaction was working against him. As I see it, those epic wars were about Satan trying with all his might to extend his heavenly position to also take territory on earth, which he will do when he is permitted to do so, but at that time he will also lose his place in the heavens and that will be a complete game changer for him. Even though Satan is restrained on earth for now it doesn't stop him trying to establish his domain here. When we look at the scale of events here, such as the holocaust, they are hard to explain without realising some scenario like this. They are the product of an epic heavenly battle where there is real suffering and many losses. Satan is here on earth but the Apostle John tells us though the Antichrist will come, presently only the spirit of Antichrist is operating here. That is because he has not been permitted to take form yet and we, or Christ in us, continues to hold him back.

As I write this it may make you think of novels that have been written and films made by people who knew something about this and used their creative talents to express it in some way, but behind it there are some actual realities.

In the end, of course, during the heavenly war/s Satan lost that attempt to take form by his own strength and it led to the long awaited re-establishment of Israel, though ironically Israel in our day is an atheistic nation, largely as a consequence of the holocaust, which, like the trials of

Job, is a hard thing for them to understand without this spiritual perspective of battle. That too is part of the preparation for the end times.

Skipping back to the main point I was making, the church, and Satan and his domain exchange positions when the rapture occurs. The saints evacuate earth and arrive in the heavenlies, and Satan loses his place in the heavenlies and arrives on earth, now with the freedom to take form and rule directly on earth, though having lost his place in the heavens he is no longer able to operate in the way he has been doing until this point, which was certainly not part of his plan. Now it has happened he must adapt his strategy and do what he must to try to win the war, but he knows now that he is in a losing position and his time is short, which means, as a creature full of pride now humiliated, he is full of bitterness and fury. What we now realise is about to happen is that God is going to judge the earth together with Satan and the whole of the evil realm who are responsible for all the evil on earth, so the evil realm is now cast down here to face the consequences of their rebellion. The time of the wrath of the Lamb is therefore as much about judgement upon Satan and the evil realm as it is upon the people of earth – not a point that is widely appreciated but one huge reason for not being here when it happens. However, despite the fact that God will begin pouring out his wrath on earth, his purposes on earth are not yet finished. First of all 144,000 have been sealed for a special purpose on earth, and secondly a huge number of people are going to realise their mistake and begin to search for God, so a multitude of people will suddenly find themselves *in the valley of decision*; one that they are positively forced to make as Satan begins to rampage through the earth using the power he now has here. Among the people left behind are all those whose hearts had grown cold towards God and were not watching, waiting and hoping for his coming as Jesus told us we need to be. For many they have turned to the things of the world and will be among those who Jesus said will be '*as in the days of Noah, eating and drinking, marrying and giving in marriage until the day Noah entered the ark*'. These are the ones who are rightly said to be 'left behind', but though what is about to come will be many times tougher for them than anything they have ever known before, their last chance has not gone, but it will now cost them absolutely everything and bring incredible hardship for them to come though it and survive. Many of these will face martyrdom for not accepting the mark of the beast.

The final point to make here about all this is that from this exchange of heavenly-earthly position it seems the raptured church may well have an important part to play in this time of wrath from their new position occupying the heavenlies as Satan once did when he formerly occupied it. In the same way that Satan used that heavenly position to tempt, deceive and oppress the people of God, so now the raptured saints may well have a role to encourage, strengthen and guide those who now turn to Christ on the earth. In this way, together with the other help God has prepared for them, the saints on earth will come though this epic time of wrath and be victorious over Satan, even though he has almost full freedom on the earth in this time. After all, Satan is the nemesis of the church so the church know him and his methods all too well. Who better to help the people of God on earth than the church who have already overcome Satan? There is a profound justice to this idea because now Satan and his cohort get a taste of their own medicine at our hand. Through these events God will again display his power in a total defeat of Satan in his battle with God's people on earth, even in these circumstances. When this age is done and dusted its purpose will be fully realised – that all creation will see and understand that nothing and no-one can rebel against God's Kingdom and prosper in any way. In this way God will use this first age of man to rule out any danger that any of his creatures will ever fall again in all eternity like both Satan and man fell in the beginning. That is why it is important this age is wrapped up so perfectly, and that is what Satan in his arrogance is continually trying to spoil. Sometimes even proving God fallible is something Satan would settle for and what keeps him going is he often thinks he is succeeding in that and it will become like the crack in the dam. But God is far more powerful than even Satan imagined and like the rest of us, he too is learning a few things about who and what God really is. This is God's plan to secure his purposes out into the reaches of eternity where we bear the testimony of this incredible age where God did what had to be done to make his creation forever secure, and he has done this great thing with the very minimum suffering possible.

Later we will take another look at Satan – who he is and what made him fall, but first we must stay on the main topic of the actual events we can expect to see as the day of the wrath of the Lamb arrives.

4. The Day of Wrath

To recap, the situation in heaven and on earth at the beginning of the day of the wrath of the Lamb are this:

- The 6th seal has been broken by the Lamb as the penultimate seal as he opens the scroll of God's wrath.

- The people of God have disappeared from the earth in the rapture and appeared before the throne and the Lamb in heaven as the Great Multitude no-one can count, who in a state of praise and worship.

- Many people have been left behind, some of whom had grown cold in their faith and begun to live for themselves, though amongst these there will be many others that have never turned to Christ but have previously heard the gospel and not responded to it.

- There has been a cataclysmic earthquake event on earth with great destruction.

- God has sealed 144,000 who have a special role during the time of wrath on the earth. They are probably all Israelites by decent, and possibly located in Israel, though initially they may be all over the world.

- Satan and the demonic realm has been cast down to the earth having lost his place as the principalities and power of the heavenly realms.

- The raptured church have now occupied the heavenly realms once occupied by Satan who used it to try to destroy them. From this position the raptured people of God may be able to perform a similar role to help the people who now turn to God on earth in the same kind of way that Satan formerly tried to hinder the church. The church may also operate against the evil beings now on earth to discourage them, to make them afraid, and to mislead them in a role reversal in order to help the people that have turned to God. If so then these will be critical times in terms of the job we have to do, and a battle, but what justice on our enemies it will be, and what victory for us!

The day of wrath is now set ready for God's wrath to be poured out, but how long will it last? What is clear is it is not literally a single day – that is just a metaphor to say it is a relatively short time. Evil will not reign on earth for long. What they think they won they will lose very quickly and it will come to an abrupt end.

When Jesus began his ministry and stood up to preach in the synagogue in Nazareth, his home town, he took the scroll of Isaiah and read Isaiah 61:2 '*I have come to proclaim the year of the Lord's favour*' at which point he stopped mid-sentence so he didn't quote the next bit that says '*...and the day of wrath.*' (Luke: 4:19). He then rolled the scroll back up, which may be significant, and gave it back, then he sat down in the synagogue and said to those there '*this day this scripture is fulfilled.*' (Luke 4:21). The important thing here is that this time of the favour of the Lord lasts a year, and the time of wrath lasts a day, metaphorically speaking. The reason Jesus stopped reading there was that this coming of his as a humble man, a carpenter, was the beginning of the time of grace that we are still living in today. John says he came '*filled with grace and truth*' (John 1:14), where grace means undeserved favour. However his second coming that Jesus himself foretold (e.g. Matt 24:37-39) would herald the beginning of another time; the day of wrath, which means the year of favour then ends and gives way to the day of wrath. This period of grace has now been around for 2000 years and counting. The day of wrath on earth will clearly be a relatively short period, like a year is to a day. In fact when it comes it will last just three and a half years.

As wrath is poured out there will be many disasters and calamities on earth and many will die. However, what is even scarier are the spiritual events on earth. The Antichrist will emerge as a man that captures the commitment of the people of the earth for many reasons – some through deception, but much of it fear. We will come to discuss him in a later chapter. Right now we need to understand something about the pressure that will then come on the people on earth to follow the Antichrist. We are told in Rev 13 about the mark of the beast, which is either his name or his number, placed on either the right hand or the forehead, without which it is not possible to either buy or sell. This means life will be extraordinarily difficult for the people of God who will only be able to get provisions to survive by trading amongst themselves, which may force them to group together, possibly in their own state/s or principalities. However that may draw the focus of the worldwide regime of the beast so they may have to maintain as much anonymity as possible. Israel it seems will be the place to which they all eventually head to try to survive, and that will lead to another cliff-hanger near the end of the days of wrath when they will be under very severe pressure of the worldwide regime of the Antichrist who is intent on destroying them so he can dominate the world.

We will discuss the meaning of 666 later, but to understand this mark of the beast more fully we first need to refer back to what is said about us, the church – the people of God, which is that all of us that belong to him have the seal of God upon us (Eph 1:13), as do the 144,000, which marks us out as God's people. As we see from Rev 7 that seal is on the forehead of the people of God. This seal is clearly a spiritual thing, not a physical thing, and it signifies that we have received the Spirit of God into our lives and we are therefore committed to him and belong to him. The fact it is on the forehead also indicates a seal and protection on the mind.

In the same way, this mark of the beast is a seal and it has a spiritual dimension to it, even if it also has a physical form as an actual mark on the body. What is clear is that this mark cannot simply be imposed on a person like placing a brand on a slave – it requires their consent. This consent is a diabolical equivalent to the commitment we have made to Christ where we invite his Spirit within. The people who take this mark will in the process be inviting and making themselves available for demonization, so one or more of the disembodied beings of the evil realm, now cast down to earth, is able to take form in the world in the same way that the Antichrist does. In just the same way our surrender to Christ requires our voluntary commitment, so the surrender to the Antichrist and the mark of the beast requires a voluntary commitment because it is a surrender of sovereignty that cannot be transferred without free consent. In fact the Antichrist may simply be a human whose physical being is the pick of the crop of persons available for demonization on earth, so Satan himself will without doubt take a human form that he judges to be the most attractive or useful to the people he wants to deceive and lead. The scary reality of the time of wrath is not just the calamities of physical judgement, but that the people who turn to God will be living in a wholly demonized world where the only exceptions to that are the people of God like themselves, or those yet to be reached and secured by the Antichrist with the mark of the beast, or brought to God by the evangelism of God's people.

In the Old Testament we see cases where God allows the evil ways of a people to reach its full depth before he judges them. This was true of Sodom and Gomorrah, and it was written to be true of the Amorites who got into some seriously heinous sinful practices. God's purpose in this whole age is to allow the full depths of evil to be seen clearly for what it truly is so he allows those realms that embrace evil to fall to the lowest levels and demonstrate the full gamut of what evil is, and what those people become who embrace it. This age of wrath is a final revelation for all eternity on what it is like to have evil completely dominating a world and as such, when all is complete, it will be an indispensable part of the record of the evil events of this world. It is likely we will look back on this age from the ages to come (eternity) like we do for the history of Israel now in the scriptures. It will stand as a permanent record of what evil is and does, and therefore tells the full story of the cost of a fall, which, alongside the other testimonies God is establishing, is what will eternally secure us against another fall.

As we see God's wrath poured out on the earth it comes to a point where it says people will no longer be able to die – i.e. to kill themselves. That is because the demons that control them will prevent it. Prior to this point death was easier for those that chose that path because the demons had their pick of other humans to possess who had taken the mark of the beast. Like a bear casting off the carcass of a hunted Salmon because he sees a better one, demons will do the same. Not only do they want to possess a human, but their hatred for them means they also have a desire to destroy them, especially believers, so they have a blood lust and these different drives are in perpetual conflict. They are like a hermit crab seeking a home and continually searching to switch for a better fit. At this point in the end times, however, their options are getting scarce because so many humans are being killed by the physical judgements God is pouring out. For the humans, by this time death will become a welcome end and release, but on earth it means each human that has the mark of the beast will start to become infested with multiple demons, or legions of them like the demoniac that Jesus met in the Gerasenes (Mark 5).

With the demoniac in the Gerasenes the demons begged Jesus not to cast them into the Abyss, which is like a terrifying prison of a multitude of demons, but to let them possess a herd of swine instead. As Jesus knew well, this was a deeply humiliating step for them because they are very proud beings and up until now they had occupied this human who is made in the image of God, thus giving them high status in the evil realm. But pigs on the other hand really do reflect the truth about evil spirits as fallen beings, which is why they seek to occupy a man because they aspire to the image of God which was their initial inducement to fall as they did with Satan right at the beginning. When they got permission from Jesus to possess the pigs they immediately forced them to run down the hillside into the lake and drown themselves, which released the demons back to the distress and discomfort of the arid disembodied state Jesus described when they have no body to occupy. But for them it was preferable to the humiliation in the evil realm of having occupied pigs, even for a moment. Now in this time of wrath, demons are beginning to fight for a place on the earth by forming cooperatives where a legion of them occupy one human. They are therefore now strongly averse to that person dying because if they lose their place there will be nowhere else for them to go. What we will see is a massive breakdown in discipline in the evil realms as demons selfishly scramble and fight each other to maintain a place on earth where they are embodied as they are desperate to be. That is why the judgement is not just one of man, but also of the whole evil realm. They are given the very thing they crave for a short time, but then judged and stripped of it by the judgements of wrath and thrust into an arena where dog-eat-dog principles would seem by comparison to be relatively civilised. Having lost their place in the heavenlies, if they also lose their place on earth they are on the verge of outer darkness with no form of expression left, so like rats on a sinking ship they will fight to maintain their place. The distress of the host human in those circumstances is unimaginable – they will be full of hatred, anger, anxiety, fear, torment, cursing and much more – something we have only glimpsed in the story of the demoniac of the Gerasenes. This is where that extremity of evil reaches its all-time zenith on the earth, just before God finally acts to draw the time of wrath to an end. At this time all the humans remaining alive that have taken the mark of the beast will only want to die. Demons always craved to occupy the earth in bodies of men made in the image of God that they could freely use for domination and sinful indulgence. In the time of wrath God has cast them down to that very place, losing their place in heaven and then also losing it on earth as the human bodies they occupy are judged, along with them. Their final situation is outer darkness with no form of expression left and no place left to go.

While this demonization of the world is taking place the people of God that have refused to take the mark of the beast and committed their lives to Christ will be gathering in one place where they make a final stand against the forces arrayed against them on earth. That place will be the land of Israel, most likely together with the 144,000 that were sealed for the purpose of helping them through the time of wrath. Though the enemy will continually press down on them as he seeks to bring the earth wholly under his occupation, the plagues of wrath will be raining down on them most likely helping the people of God when they most need it. And just like it did for the Israelites in those days in Egypt, those plagues will not rain on their land. The plagues of Egypt were only a reflection or *foreshadow* of this end time event, but this is the real deal to which all of that was pointing. God continues to fight for them right up to the final cliff-hanger when the day is nearly lost. Like Pharaoh in that day, the evil powers of the earth will continue to press forward in their determination to destroy God's people which will draw them to their own destruction. Then comes the last and final intervention of God – which some who read the Book of Revelation have mistaken to be the rapture having not realised the difference between the tribulation and the time of wrath, and the fact that the rapture actually occurs earlier on the breaking of the 6th seal at the point of transition.

I refer there to the events prophesied of Armageddon, and the final harvest at the end of Rev 14, but for now we need to examine the Antichrist further.

5. The Antichrist

The spirit of Antichrist is already at work in the world and has been since the fall of man. However the full manifestation of the physical person of the Antichrist is yet to come. At the moment it is Christ in the world that restrains the Antichrist from coming and taking form in this way (2 Thes 2:7). He would take form if he could, and he has tried warring against God to win the means to do so, but despite some epic struggles he has so far failed, other than as something like a guerrilla war where he is not the ruling power in possession of the territory of earth. God, and Christ in us, will continue to battle against him to restrain him until the right time. When that time comes Christ will be raptured out of the world – meaning the people of God who have Christ within them will be taken out, and at the same time Satan will be forced out of the heavenly realms and down to the earth losing that position in the heavenlies that he has operated in for so long. Then, with no prayers and intercessions of the saints any longer protecting this domain on earth, or any ministry of deliverance, he will be free to occupy the earth where he will persuade the masses to follow him, surrender to him, and take his mark. When they make this surrender they will open the way to be demonized. The Antichrist himself will be a person that is demonized by Satan himself at this time and he will choose the person and the body that will best serve his purposes, which means the person he judges to be best suited to persuading the world to follow him. That was a recap.

Let's now take a look at what the Antichrist will be like, and what his regime will look like. To get into this we are going to take a look at a relevant chapter in the book of Daniel – Dan 7, the vision of the four beasts.

Some of the dreams and visions in the Book of Daniel are clearly prophecies foretelling the regimes that are to come and they have a chronology to them. Take for instance the first dream (Dan 2) of King Nebuchadnezzar who Daniel was educated and prepared to serve, along with all the other wise men, including his three Jewish companions – Shadrak, Meshak and Abednego.

Daniel came to prominence in the Babylonian Kingdom as a consequence of his interpretation of this dream in Dan 2. It was a dream of a statue with a gold head, silver arms and torso, bronze belly and thighs, legs of iron, and feet of a mixture of iron and baked clay. From our point in history this prophecy from around 570 BC can be clearly seen to accurately predict the sequence of empires that have ruled the world – Babylonian, Medes and Persians, Greek, Romans, Fragmentation of the Roman Empire which persists in Europe to this day. The prophecy was given at the time of the first of these, when the Babylonian empire was in place. The same is true of other parts of Daniel's prophecies, for example the vision of the Ram and Goat in Dan 8 – they can be seen to have a definite place in history. For that reason many have tried to identify the Kingdoms described by the four beasts in Dan 7 in the same way but have found this just doesn't seem to fit into what we know of history in quite the same way. Of course a good effort has been made, but rather than the Cinderella eureka moment of Dan 2 with the huge statue where the glass slipper clearly fits, we get a kind of ugly sister experience where nothing seems to fit properly without 'shoehorning' it in, so we have our doubts about the interpretation. That's because this is not just a repeat of Dan 2 in another form, as some think – it is something else and it has another purpose.

The four beasts in Daniel define all the types of kingdom or empire that can be found in this world. By types of kingdom I mean the different fundamental principles on which these regimes operate. Every nation on earth and throughout history can be seen to fall into one or other of these categories.

The aim of any worldly government is to govern or rule the people in a way that the ruling entity keeps order, and establishes and maintains its power. In other words they seek to somehow control the behaviour of the people under it to make sure the government maintains its rule. This requires the conformity of the people and there are several fundamental ways by which that conformity can be secured. That brings us to the symbols of the four beasts which show us exactly what those various methods are. Or rather the first three show us all the fundamentals. The last beast is special, having characteristics of the others, but it relates only to the time of the end.

Lion – The first beast is a lion with eagles' wings. As Daniel watched its wings were torn off, and it was left standing on its two hind feet, like a human being. And it was given a human mind.

The lion, with its regal mane and the pride around it, is a symbol of kingship and majesty, and is frequently used as a symbol for that purpose. It is a communal animal living in a pride that has a strict hierarchy and leader. The symbol speaks of a powerful animal, so it has some strength which translates in human governmental terms as having military armies. The principle of a king is to command the respect of the people and thereby to rule by securing their voluntary commitment based on their belief in him, and reverent fear of him. The people believe in their king. He therefore has to be seen as a good ruler, with wisdom, uprightness and fairness. It is this image with the people that keeps him in control. When kings come to be seen as corrupt, they fall. As long as the people see him as a force for good his position is secure so he (or she) is careful to maintain that image before the people.

We can point to many monarchies of the past that have run on this principle. Of course today there are still a few monarchies but among the larger nations of the world these have become more figureheads than true monarchies where power resides. They still operate on that principle of commanding respect and admiration from the people but they run alongside some sort of parliament that actually rules for them. That is where the rest of this symbolism comes into play.

First of all let's make the point that this symbolic lion has wings. Wings speak of an empire. The wings spread and provide transport over large regions covering a large or vast area. They also cover as they spread which symbolises the covering and protection a king extends to his subjects, wherever they may be.

All of Europe had monarchies like this of some kind – England, France, Spain, Portugal, Holland, Prussia, Russia etc. – and these monarchies all made efforts to establish an empire. In fact as time went by England formed a union and became Britain and then went on to establish the largest empire ever known which covered a quarter of the area of the globe and a third of the people of the world. Its residue still exists in the form of the Commonwealth of Nations that still work together in some exclusive ways even now. The fact that the lion had wings is an indication that the monarchies of the world would spread their wings and expand into empires. The fact that those wings came to be torn off and the lion would stand up on its hind legs shows those monarchies would transform into something else, and they would lose their empires. That something else turns out to be democracies, with parliaments, where the lion is made to stand up in a way that resembles a man, and is given the heart of a man.

Man is a moral being, not a beast. What this suggests is these monarchies would try hard to become more moralistic in form, rather than always ruling by the dictation of royal edict, so morality is its guiding principle. This is really the main concern of all modern democracies. They have the same goals as the original king, to rule, but have come to be ruled by the people for the people with a symbolic monarchy doing little but overlooking it, at best. It has the advantage that the king can distance himself from the bad decisions of the parliament and always be seen to be in favour of its subjects. However, despite all its efforts, what this is saying is it is still a monarchical beast underneath even though it tries hard to be seen and operate as a moral man. Presidents and prime ministers do in truth still operate to some degree like kings, even though they have a concern to always maintain that perception of morality.

The main reason this migration to democracy has taken place is simply that time and history has shown us that no man is really up to the task of ruling as a king. Too often power has been shown to corrupt, or that kings have lacked the wisdom to rule well so it has had to pass to the people who can make a better job of it by doing it together, as difficult as that sometimes is. If it were possible to be ruled by a truly wise and benevolent king that could not be corrupted by power, then this could possibly be an idyllic situation, with less conflict than any other type of rule. However, the rule of Solomon was specifically given to show us that even the wisest on this earth can be corrupted by power in the end, and come to need the discipline of God like all others.

Bear – the second beast is a bear. In terms of a type of human government it stands for shear brute force. People are ruled in this kingdom by oppression. If they don't conform they suffer, so they conform, or die at the hands of the government. Of course when we think of a bear as a symbol, Russia is the first place that comes to mind, which ironically has given us the perfect example of this kind of rule, though of course we can point to many more. The bear is seen to have ribs in its mouth and it devours the flesh of many people. Regimes of this kind are brutal. They exact a toll of blood on their people if they don't toe the line, or sometimes even if they do. The leader is not nearly as concerned about their moral image with the people as the monarchical lion. Fear, or terror, is their motivator, not respect, so they are more concerned that the people properly fear them than respect them. The bear too is a powerful animal so again it has military forces at its command. These forces may be for defence of the realm, but they are invariably also used as a means of implementing their oppression on their own people.

One point to note is that the bear does not have wings which indicates no significant empire. Generally to maintain an empire by brute force seems to have its limits because it requires a vast effort and huge resources. Then at every opportunity the people rise up to throw off oppression if it can so it never lasts too long. Britain managed a lasting empire using the monarchical lion model by convincing the people that it was there for their own benefit. That is much cheaper and easier to rule, if you can pull it off. Some even joined the British Empire voluntarily. India would be the prime example where 350 million people were ruled by a few tens of thousands of foreigners for more than 200 years. Once they mutated to show more bear like qualities that particular rule soon came to an end. It was Gandhi's genius that provoked and revealed that, and changed the perception of the Indian people towards the British which soon brought it to a swift end. In any case Britain was not prepared to go any further down that road as it had already made moves towards democracy so it had to let go of India against its will after a very minimal struggle to retain power. Had Gandhi challenged a true bear he would simply have been eaten, though no doubt the people would have risen up to throw off oppression.

Leopard – the third beast is a leopard. Again this symbolises another way in which a government may seek to rule its people that is fundamentally different to both of the previous two.

The leopard is an animal of stealth. It operates in cunning and crafty ways using deception to rule the people. By convincing the people of their special status as a ruler they secure their commitment and service. Most of these regimes take the form of someone claiming divinity, or they promote some form of ideology, or something like that, and then on the basis of that they demand the voluntary obedience of the people to conform to their rule. For a ruler who claims divinity they may orchestrate some kind of deceptive display of their power to prove their claim and make the people believe in them. Or the belief of the people may be established purely on the back of some kind of myth about them which the regime takes steps to disseminate.

By far the most common form of this type of regime is where the people are led to believe their ruler is divine. As God, or as his appointed representative, they lay claim to the submission and obedience of the people who may even be required to die to protect them.

This leopard has four wings, again symbolising the fact it will spread to form empires. That it has multiple pairs of wings suggests multiple different empires based on this same principle of deception, though no doubt each based on a different myth.

The leopard also has four heads suggesting that there are four distinct manifestations of this kind of regime. That may not mean four government leaders, but based on the fact this is dealing with principles rather than specific regimes, it may mean four different kinds of deception where only one of them is the claim to divinity. For example another kind of deception may be a witchdoctor kind of rule where the one that rules is believed to have special powers – often this would require some kind of deceptive acts of magic or wonder. A third could be based purely on image or personality where the leader is basically the fairest or cleverest of them all and demands submission on that basis. A fourth could simply be a false religion with its priesthood that rules and its codes of conduct with promises of rewards and punishments to secure the conformity of the people.

All beasts – In all of these cases we can look around, or look back into history, and see examples. Let's name a few: The Roman Emperors that proclaimed themselves divine and made an empire from it; Japan's Hirohito who was believed divine and sought an empire from it; Islam as a complete religion with its political priesthood that has formed empires in the past and still seeks to do so; Christianity has operated in similar ways in the past where it has been turned into a political religion and means to control the people, despite the truth in its literature;

Communist ideology could be considered one of these given that it includes a belief in atheism. The list of cases is actually endless and it can be seen operating at many levels down to the rule of small tribes in Africa to multinational empires involving many peoples and countries.

In truth none of the actual regimes in the world operate purely on just one of these three different principles. Rather they are a mixture of them all in some measure but invariably they lean heavily towards one of them. Sometimes regimes switch from one form to another, so for example we have often seen a lion monarchy migrate very quickly into a brutal bear in order to maintain power once they have lost the respect of the people. A leopard running on stealth may do a similar thing if its myth is exposed and belief is lost. We see this in Islam, political Christianity and in Communism when it begins to break down. Unfortunately for these rulers it is a difficult thing to maintain more than one of these kinds of regimes at the same time. If a monarchy want to suppress dissenters with brutal elements they have to carefully conceal it or somehow distance themselves from it so they don't appear to the people to be the one to blame. That kind of balancing act is hard to maintain, but this is exactly the kind of masterful operation we expect to see in the end times from the beast in the Book of Revelation, the Antichrist, when he comes to rule the earth, as we will see. In fact the last beast in Daniel's vision was very frightening to him because it was something unfamiliar and much more fearsome than the rest. Fundamentally it was bear-like in form – an oppressor, but its brutality was on a whole different level to the bear. It was also unnatural with its strength, its iron teeth, its bronze claws, and its behaviour of stamping down and crushing its victims under its feet. What is clear from the text is all these kingdoms are still in existence at the end (Dan 7:12) so they are not simply a sequential set of kingdoms like Nebuchadnezzar's statue in Dan 2. They all exist together, but the fourth most frightening beast seems to appear at the end to suppress and subdue them all by its brutality. What comes after this final beast is it is overthrown by the coming of God's Kingdom, which is something still be discussed, but that is a lower priority at the moment so let's continue for a while to look at the events that will happen on the earth before that during the times of tribulation and then wrath.

There is a clear alignment between Daniel's description of the last of the four beasts, and John's description of the beast in Revelation that is boastful and proud. But before this in the Book of Revelation there is a very strong alignment of these two in Rev 13:2 – *This beast looked like a leopard, but it had the feet of a bear and the mouth of a lion*. What this is saying is this beast will operate in some way using the principles of all the other three beasts of Daniel that we have already discussed. The mouth of the lion – he speaks like king. Feet like a bear – he oppresses the people and devours their flesh but does it differently to the bear by crushing rather than eating. He looked like a leopard – he is a beast of stealth so he deceives the people, maybe by elevating himself to divine status, maybe by special powers, maybe by making a new religion – which may be an anti-God religion, and maybe by all of that. That is the true form and nature of the Antichrist when he comes and begins to rule the earth in the time of God's wrath.

To round this off let me tell you my feelings about this scripture in Dan 7. For me, as a revelation of what we see, it stands in the same bracket as Dan 2 and Nebuchadnezzar's vision of the huge statue representing the empires to come. That chapter of Dan 2 is so accurate to what we know of history, even though it is so clear it was written only in the time of the first kingdom mentioned, that it becomes a huge validation of the accuracy of Bible prophecy. There we have what I called a Cinderella eureka moment when we see the glass slipper fits perfectly. When it comes to Dan 7 and we try to fit that into the same history we don't quite get the same experience. Instead, as I said before, it is like an ugly sister fit where we are shoehorning history into it − until we come to this interpretation. Then we get another delightful Cinderella moment because the symbols it uses not only describes the fundamentals of every known kingdom, it even looks forward into the modern day with its view of democracy, giving us perfect symbols to describe what we now see in our populated modern world. But these are not the only instances of scripture that delight us like this. Another I will come to later before we finish, just for the delight of it, where we again take a look at the horsemen of the apocalypse and see how much that too fits with what we now know of history that was clearly impossible to know at the time of writing.

In truth, when we look at this definition of the different fundamentals for ruling we see this applies not just to nations, but to every form of worldly institution. That includes businesses and other organisations − and it emphatically applies to churches. We see each one of these kinds of rule taking place in churches, but they are all worldly in nature − even the lion/king model. For church we were intended to run on a very different model to anything the world has which is based on God's rules by his Spirit through all members, so Christ is the head of the church. That was lost after the early church and at some point is set to be recovered in these last days, for which reason I was led to write a book about it − *The Original*

Church to Come. In the interim we suffer all the problems of trying to run church under one of these worldly models, which really does explain the shortcomings of church as we know it in our day. In each case there is a head displacement that replaces the Spirit and removes the part all members should be taking in the body. The kind of church we should be operating allows all members to participate throughout, as they are led, and they are led by their overseers to test all things. It is that open testing that once protected the church from false teachings, and false apostles who would exploit them. Nowadays this is not done and all of these find their way into the church without a challenge, giving opportunity to all these worldly forms of church, and opening the door to false teaching and false prophecy. Ideally something like this whole message should be weighed by the whole body to discern what is actually from the Lord, as should be done for everything else. Then the deceiver will be defeated. Right now we have delegated that responsibility to our leaders, but that is not the way it was originally, or should be now.

As a final look at the Antichrist, let's take a look at his famous number, 666. What does it mean? We are told in Revelation that it is possible to calculate the meaning of the number of his name, and there has been a whole lot of speculation about that ever since. Here I will simply offer my thoughts on it.

I suspect the designation of 666 to the Antichrist as the number of his name has considerable depth. However, one rule of thumb for me with interpreting all prophecy is to first find the simple and obvious interpretation. When things get highfalutin then for me that is a warning it is off track. It is just this kind of simplicity that I find so convincing in Dan 2 and Dan 7, and as you will see later in Rev 6 and the four horsemen. We see the same kind of thing in the whole study of maths when it interprets our physical world. Take for example Einstein's famous equation E=mc². It is the simplest equation but as physicists will tell you its implications are vast, keeping many scientists busy and working for the whole of their lives. That is the power and wonder of maths. We find the same for Isaac Newton and his discovery of the laws of motion that were used to predict the path of the planets. His equations were equally simple, but had a profound effect. As a trained and qualified Mechanical Engineer I discovered the power of maths and was always awed by it. A Mechanical Engineer is actually an applied mathematician such that 90% of the course is maths, and in the final year it was 100% maths. We use it to interpret the real world, process it, and then interpret back a results that predict or explain something to us. Often the indication that we were on the right track was its simplicity. As some have said, God is clearly a mathematician – but he is also the very maker of the phenomenon of maths. I suppose we should not therefore be surprised when he offers us the odd numerical conundrum to chew on – as our parent he likes to stretch us and challenge us a bit.

A good starting place would be to look at God's number which would be 777, in the same way that 666 represents the Antichrist. We are told God's Spirit is a seven-fold spirit. Not seven spirits, but a seven-fold Spirit. In Spirit he is a unity of seven aspects. Equally we also know he is a unity of three persons – Father, Son and Spirit – which is the reason there are three sevens in that number. Each seven represents one of those persons, each perfect and in unity with the others. Of course as we know this is all part of the mystery of God because he is one being, even though he presents himself as three persons. God is one. He is a unity. There is no division in him. All of this expression is of perfect harmony and unity. It is a marvellous mystery for us because God is so much greater as a being than we are with his multiple forms. When we come to God we too share that *one* Spirit so we become part of that unity. Then as we all grow up in our faith we proceed towards a unity of faith (Eph 4:13) – we come to see the truth and be united in it. All of this means the number 7 perfectly represents God. First because it is a prime number, which means it is indivisible. Of course 2, 3, and 5 are also prime numbers. Apart from 2 all other even numbers are not prime precisely because they are divisible by two. For the odd numbers 7 is the highest single digit prime before we get to one that is divisible – which is 9, divisible by 3. God's number is therefore the highest single digit prime in our decimal number system after which we move into double digits, but God is one, so that single digit 7 represents him well. The number 777 is therefore a combination of two primes – 3 and 7 – where the three sevens each represent one of the persons in which God presents himself to us – Father, Son, and Spirit, each of them perfect. In short, it all speaks to me of the indivisible unity of God.

Now to consider the number 6. First it falls short of 7 and in this respect it reflects the truth about Satan. He aspired to become '*as the most high*' and to be worshipped like God, but he fell short of that mark. Whereas 7 is God's number and speaks of perfection and holiness, so 6 speaks of falling short of that and so it represents imperfection – evil, corruption. Then whereas 7 is a prime and so indivisible, 6 has a unique property of *all numbers* which is that it is supremely divisible. By that I mean every number up to half way (the max point) can be used to divide 6 – it is divisible by 1, 2, and 3. No other number can possibly have this boast. What that speaks of is real divisibility – Satan's kingdom is the very opposite of united. That is not surprising because he is not like God in that he can fill all those that belong to him and so bring them into unity. Satan's kingdom is full of selfish individuals that each have their own selfish agenda. He unites them only by managing their self-interest, by promise of reward, or by threat, but fundamentally Satan is profoundly divided – and that will ultimately be the downfall of his kingdom. The fact there a three sixes in 666, mean Satan is again trying to emulate God by coming in three forms. He is first Satan, second Antichrist, and then we see him coming in a third form in Revelation as the statue of the beast that lived and astounded the people. Part of Satan's falling short of God is that he masquerades as God, as divine, and so he deceives the people. God is entirely true, but Satan is a liar in every way – a shape shifter – a leopard – a deceiver. That's why Jesus said lying is Satan's native language – he invented it, and became the master of the art of it.

The next good question to ask is why then will Satan use this number to represent himself when the day of the Antichrist comes along given that we all know what it stands for. The answer is, as a deceiver he will redefine it, and I see that redefinition already out there. He will probably say 6 is the number of man and the three 666's together speak of the perfect man, which is what he will present himself as, probably at the same time choosing a stunningly attractive body to present himself – unlike Jesus who had no form that would naturally attract us to him (Is 53:2). In effect he replaces God with man. The world as we know it is already fixed on image and this is something the Antichrist will exploit. Part of his deception is to redefine things like 666 to use it in his favour, but we should remember what it really speaks of is he is evil and corrupt, and he has fallen short of God, despite his deceptive appearance/s.

As I said when I began discussing his number, 666 may have more depth with other meanings so other ideas may still be valid, but for me at this point, this is the major meaning of it.

6. Satan

Now we have taken a look at the Antichrist and the kind of regime he will set up on earth, we should also take a brief look at Satan and who he is. As generals in wars tell us, it is best to know your adversary. That helps us to anticipate his moves and so prepare ourselves for them.

The Antichrist is a manifestation of Satan on earth. That would be the shortest and most accurate definition. But who was Satan in the beginning?

He may have been an archangel. Altogether there may have been seven archangels, though I'm not certain on that. The book of Enoch is not accepted as part of our cannon of scripture, but it is nevertheless quoted in the book of Jude and in 2 Peter. There are in fact three books of Enoch but only the first is quoted. When we look at the parts quoted it does relate particularly to the fall of angels from heaven who came and corrupted the earth in their own self-interest, and then they appealed back to God for forgiveness and reinstatement but were denied as no way was possible for their redemption. That part is referred to in the Bible (2 Peter 2:4) and it should be a chilling revelation to us as we too have fallen as a result of their influence on us, but for us God has made a way, though at great expense, for us to be redeemed. One thing we must always remind ourselves of is even the possibility of redemption for man is a very difficult thing to accomplish, even for God, but for us he has done what is necessary even though no way was possible for fallen angels.

If Satan was an archangel it seems he may have been over the order of angels we know as cherubim, who seem to be guardians. Many people have lots of ideas about this, but things are not so certain. We also have to be aware the Bible warns us that this can become an aspect of spiritual vanity for some people – to be an expert on the angelic realms. I prefer to stick to what is intimated in scripture and leave it at that, unless I get some specific revelations which I will have to treat with caution.

The verses in Ezekiel 28:13-19 & Isaiah 14:12-19 seem to speak of a guardian cherub of immense beauty that was in Eden, who determined himself to become '*as the most high*' and fell into corruption and wickedness. Though it is written in the context of kingdoms in those days, these scriptures seem to have multiple meaning including reference to someone who is of heavenly origins. Most believe this is Satan, in which case he was a guardian cherub, and most probably the archangel over the whole order of guardian angels – the cherubim. Other orders of angels seem to exist where Michael is the archangel over all warrior angels, Gabriel is the archangel of all messenger angels, and then there are the seraphim – another order of angel whose primary focus seems to be worship and direct ministry to God, who no doubt also have an archangel serving over them. When we think of our very guardians betraying God's trust in them and corrupting mankind for their own purposes then we see this was not a sin of deception, as it was for man, but a deliberate and informed act and decision of will, which makes it abundantly clear why no way back can be found for them.

My personal view from the Ezekiel text is that this guardian cherub may have been the most beautiful creature God created. For that reason when his vanity got the better of him he saw himself as someone who could aspire to be like God. Had there been another angel more beautiful he may not have fallen as he did, but it seems he was the most glorious and therefore the prime candidate to make this kind of assumption. It is also most likely that he developed a way to conceal that wickedness, given that in heaven all things are normally revealed, not concealed. That is why Jesus referred to him as the author of lies, and said lying is his native language. In the end wickedness was found in him (Ez 28:15) and he was cast out of heaven, along with many of his order that followed him, becoming trapped between heaven and earth as the principalities and powers of the air.

In his now darkened and corrupted state Satan has become a formidable foe to us, having intelligence way in advance of anything we possess. However angels do protect us in the earthly realm and we too are given authority to wield against him as this is our God given domain, not his. We are therefore part of the restraining force that keeps Satan at bay on earth and denies him the freedom to manifest himself in an unrestricted way. Sometimes men give him opportunity by delegating their authority to him, and this leads to a whole lot of trouble on earth, but generally it is the people of God that exercise restraining power along with the warring angels to keep him at bay. This is a state of affairs that will continue until we are taken out of the way, though it doesn't prevent Satan from mounting significant attacks that seek to extend his territory to earth at times, but he is not yet the ruling power here.

Now Satan has fallen he has become a master deceiver. He is still full of pride and arrogance, which is often his downfall as it drives him impatiently on. Equally the fallen evil beings in his kingdom have similar motivation which actually puts them all in competition with each other in a predatory way, with hierarchies, but they are smart enough to know they are stronger by forming cooperatives so there are alliances made in their own self-interest with other evil beings in order to gain some advantage in their realm together – hence we see cases like the demoniac of the Gerasenes mentioned earlier, who had a legion of demons. As these evil beings, including Satan, are no longer indwelt by God they have become totally selfish. Satan therefore has to rule them by controlling their self-interest. For them the whole idea of self-sacrifice is not something they would contemplate and were probably utterly astonished by the fact Jesus was ready to make such a sacrifice on our behalf to redeem us. Frequently the competitive selfish nature of demons means they act in their own interest, and only in the interest of the whole when forced to do so. This causes them make big mistakes when it comes to battle, and Satan is hard pushed to control it, even by threats of punishment and oppression. The nature of Satan and the evil realm is anger, hatred and cursing. They are destroyers of all that is good by nature. They are proud and they are jealous, both of us/man and of each other. They know they are headed for destruction but they nevertheless act in desperation in the faint hope they will find a way to persist in this universe somehow.

I was always a great fan of J.R.R. Tolkien's fantasy novel – *The Lord of the Rings*. Mainly because it embodies his knowledge of these evil realms and how they work in a remarkable way, and they are compared to how the realms of good operate by laying aside their self-interest for a higher purpose. The films were great of course, but the books contain numerous additional nuggets that the films didn't cover showing these aspects of the good and evil realms. Through this, and many works of art, this generation is quite well informed of what evil is and how it operates. However the ultimate real deal will be when the real forces behind these fantasies begin to finally manifest themselves in our domain on earth. Then things are likely to get really scary.

7. Who Is Left Behind

Once we get into the day of wrath beyond the breaking of the 6th seal in The Book of Revelation, there are many mentions of the people of God present on the earth through the outpouring of wrath on creation, and through the time of the beast and his mark. But if the church is raptured at that point, then who exactly are they?

First of all it seems there are 144,000 sealed on earth for a special purpose. These it says are descendants of the tribes of Israel. We have no reason not to take that literally, even though the Jewish people today do not really know what tribe they belong to. It seems these are the very people Paul was referring to when he wrote about the remnant have been chosen by grace and have not bowed their knee to Baal (Rom 11:5). These are reserved for a special ministry on earth when the time of wrath comes. They may be based in Israel, or they may be spread around the globe and gather to Israel in the time of wrath to avoid Satan's attacks.

A personal view is that these were the people Satan was trying to destroy during the WW2 holocaust, or the ones from whom they will descend, because they will be so instrumental in his defeat at the end. Like Herod tried to wipe out Jesus as a babe, so Satan tried to wipe out these special ones in a pre-emptive strike. In the end it may have been the impatience of the demonic force driving Hitler that led to the loss of the war – sometimes God leads Satan by misinformation and it makes him act foolishly, which is sometimes why we too have only part of the full picture – so that Satan can't find out from us what is really going on – for that reason we have to accept only knowing in part like the soldiers on the battlefield compared to their commander.

Hitler's move into Russia was a huge mistake for sure, primarily motivated by the fact there were so many Jews in that region which he wanted to destroy. Of course the Jews themselves see none of this because they don't recognise Jesus as their Messiah, and they don't have the Book of Revelation in their accepted divine literature. The holocaust is therefore a huge mystery to them – why God didn't protect them from it? They are blind to the fact there is a war going on in the heavens over them so the result is today many have turned atheist and abandoned their Jewish faith altogether.

This ignorance of who Jesus is and their perplexity on events aligns with what Paul told us is happening – that Israel has experienced a hardening in part until the full number of gentiles have come to faith in Jesus (Rom 11:25-31). Here again we see a timeclock based on a people count. There is a specific number of gentiles that must come to Christ before Israel becomes significantly impacted with the gospel of Christ and comes to recognise him as their Messiah that they have so long been waiting for. When this happens it will be the sign of the fig tree putting forth its leaves that Jesus spoke about – the fig tree being a symbol of the nation of Israel, and this will be a key sign of the end. Of course since 1948 Israel has been re-established as a nation, incredibly, again mainly as a consequence of the holocaust, so there we see the plan of the enemy backfiring in a big way, which it often does. Some believe that re-establishment of the nation is the fig tree putting forth its leaves, but I believe there also has to be a point where they realise their mistake and turn to Christ as their true Messiah – when they mourn for the one they pierced (Zech 12:10). That point may come very near the end of this day of favour we are in now – the day of grace.

Beyond the 144,000 in the day of wrath there will be many that are not watching and waiting for the second coming of Christ that he promised and these will be like the foolish virgins in Matthew 25 that miss the coming of the bride groom. Jesus said to them 'I never knew you' – they are ones that never developed a relationship with him in the day of favour, the day of grace.

There will also be some like Lots wife whose hope and desire is set here in this world and in this life, so they look back. This will include some that do know Jesus and have a relationship with him. They lost their vision of the heavenly destiny, or never had it, and got attached to this earth and all it has to offer. These are the ones that will look back when disaster strikes. God is looking for those whose faith and vision is not for this life, but for a better city, as Abraham's was (Heb 11:10).

When I look around at various people with the various different hopes they have, there are a few sects that show this kind of vision that is earth bound. Some believe the apocalypse already happened in the decade from 70AD and so have set their hopes here on earth. Others are expecting God to take them through the time of wrath believing it is all part of the tribulation we all have to pass through. For all of these I believe they will be staying for the time of wrath and won't realise their mistake until they find themselves left behind and having to face it. Among them are many Jehovah's Witnesses who have a certain expectation of what is going to happen, but I believe some of this is seriously misguided.

Jehovah's Witnesses divide their people into two groups –
those with a heavenly hope, and those with an earthly
hope. They believe for those with a heavenly hope there
are only 144,000 people, which they realise is a low
number out of 8 million followers so the vast majority of
their people have an earthly hope. When the JWs take
communion all those with an earthly hope pass the
communion cup on without drinking because they consider
the cup to be only for those that have a heavenly hope. I
am still astounded that this should happen because by the
true meaning of the cup what they are affirming is they are
not part of the body of Christ, and therefore set not for
salvation, but for wrath. They also interpret the whole idea
of 'born again' as Jesus spoke of it in John 3 as for those
that have a heavenly hope when they go to heaven, but
actually Jesus said born again is an earthly thing if you
look closely (John 3:12), meaning it happens on earth even
though it is spiritual and from heaven. The JWs have
therefore both bypassed the salvation of God and bypassed
the cup that symbolises and confesses it. I have no doubt
therefore that these have been set up to miss the rapture
and pass into the time of wrath they have been so fixed
upon, but I expect when the rapture occurs many of them
will realise their mistake and turn to Christ for real for the
first time. These will then be part of the people of God that
have to come through the time of wrath and will be
victorious over the beast, refusing his mark, even at the
cost of their lives.

Having said all that, I still believe there is a kernel of truth
in the ideas of either an earthly or heavenly hope. Those
that come to salvation in this present time of favour
become part of the body of Christ – the bride of Christ
whose place is with Christ in the New Jerusalem –
Heaven. This is in their hearts. However, those that come
through the time of wrath have a different destiny that is

here on this earth. They therefore pass on though the millennium era to what lies beyond on earth. We therefore do indeed have two classes of people with different destinies, and only one of them seems to be the Bride of Christ.

What I find is those that belong to that heavenly destiny have a hope and vision that welcomes heaven and is set upon it. But often for those that do not have a heavenly hope but an earthly one, they may not realise what they are choosing but some of them will in the end win through the time of wrath to find that earthly destiny. My main concern for those people is that some of them have the idea that everything on earth will be rosy despite the apocalyptic scriptures, whereas in fact it will for a time be like shear hell on earth with immense suffering, and I think in those times they may come to regret their mistake, but they may also be the ones to lead many others to be faithful to Christ through those times once they realise the scenario they are into of wrath and judgement. When that happens I doubt these people will be quite so enamoured with the leaders who led them there, most of whom will probably be there with them. I think when some of these come to face the music they will wish they had stuck to the orthodox view, rather than the progressive one, and stayed watchful and hopeful for the coming of the Lord.

Now for these in the time of wrath, they will be helped by the 144,000 that have been sealed to lead them through it; they will be helped by the church that now occupy the heavenlies in the way Satan once did; and they will be helped by the plagues God will be pouring out on their enemies that will slow or halt their attack on earth. Victory in the end is likely to be a real cliff-hanger but those that hold fast to their faith in God will pull through it as Israel did when the plagues were poured out on Egypt. Satan, like Pharaoh, will be destroyed as he pursues the people of God in this time through his pride and arrogance that always drive him on to make his mistakes.

8. Accuracy of Bible Prophecy

This is a chapter I promised earlier when delighting in the accuracy of the symbols in Dan 2 and Dan 7 that fit so well into our modern world, even though those words were written way before much of it came into being. As I said before, they are a huge point of validation for the accuracy of Bible prophecy, but they are far from the only scriptures that hit that mark. That said there are still huge swathes of Bible prophecy that need to be revealed to us for us to get the full meaning, but seeing parts of the scripture like these unfold so well helps us believe they are as accurate even though we don't know their meaning, and that God will reveal their meaning in his time when we need it. Right now, in the interests of inspiring us further on the value of prophecy, I want to take another look at the scriptures on the four horsemen of the apocalypse, so called, by comparing that scriptures in Rev 6 to a passage in the Old Testament – Zechariah 6.

One point I made repeatedly earlier is the horsemen belong to this/our present era, which is the era of tribulation, so strictly speaking these horsemen should probably be known as the horsemen of the tribulation.

Of course some sceptics would level the criticism that the Apostle John knew the Zechariah scriptures when he wrote the Book of Revelation so he may be purposely just continuing the theme rather than writing a revelation as he saw it. But once again the great thing about this, like Dan 7, is that it has parts that fit so well into our modern world in a way that the authors of either of these texts could never have anticipated. Let's take a look at these scriptures.

In Rev 6 we get the breaking of the seals where each of the first four seals are the releasing of the horsemen of the apocalypse, and each horse we are told has a different colour. In Zech 6 we get another scene involving horses of the same or equivalent colour.

One thing I learned about Bible symbols and prophecy is that there is a huge consistency in its use of symbols across the board. That is something you have to study for yourself to appreciate and it is something else that can really heighten your faith in the accuracy of scripture as words that are sourced in God – so it is well worth doing. In this case the correlation is unmistakable and we would be surprised if two texts should have such similar images and not have some relevance or relation to each other. When we combine these two scriptures we find it raises questions, but it also gives us more information that paints a fuller picture, so that is what we will do. It's not really for the purpose of advancing our knowledge – though others may disagree, but as I said it helps us to realise the scriptures are inspired and have a convincing handle on real modern day events.

When it comes to the horsemen let's be clear that these are something released by God. That does not mean God does the work, but that he releases the evil forces in the world that go out to do their work. As I have repeatedly said, this part of the apocalypse is not judgement or the day of wrath. It is tribulation. Everything God does is a holy act. He is not some kind of tyrant. God has made clear that this age of evil is on a time limit, but that time will and must run out. Jesus has bought time for a while, which is the present day of favour during which he reaches out to reap a harvest of men back to God, but this cannot be a permanent state of affairs. Evil and corruption must be addressed and it must be done in a perfect way that shows

God to be entirely holy and just. I said it before, and wrote a whole book about it – God is using this fall to prevent there ever being a repeat of it in the ages to come – eternity. From it will come all the protection we need to be secure as free willed beings in eternity, who live with numerous other free willed beings that have all learned the same lessons that we have. God even wants to trust us with great power in those ages to come so our training must be robust – then we will not be vulnerable to fall like Satan was in the beginning.

When John opens his vision of heaven in the book of Revelation (Rev 4) he describes four '*living creatures*' before the throne, each with eyes all over their body and a different face – Lion, Ox, Man, Eagle. These represent the whole of God's creation and they have authority over it. It is one of these four living creatures that calls forth each of the four horsemen in turn, showing they are giving them authority to do what they are about to do in the earth.

Those who see these riders like the dark riders in *Lord of the Rings* may not have realised these are messengers from God, not Satan. They are necessary for the winding up of the age. Satan has no power to simply step forward and do such things as these. For now he is trapped between heaven and earth, desperately trying to advance his domination, but so far prevented from doing so by Christ in the earth who restrains him. His only opportunities are where men lend him their God given authority in the earth for evil purpose, but there are many on earth that limit his activity through their prayers, intercessions and deliverance ministries. Jesus taught us all to pray '*your kingdom come on earth as it is in heaven*', and '*deliver us from evil*'. All of that amounts to men using their authority to keep evil back. But now those restraints are being purposely reduced as we approach the end of the age so these evils begin to be released and manifest in the earth.

As Rev 6 reads, when each of the first four seals of the scroll are broken, one of the living creatures says 'Come' and one of the horsemen comes forth to do their work, according to their colour – White, Red, Black and Green.

As these seals are opened and the horsemen are released, though judgement has not yet come, tremors of that coming judgement and the day of wrath to come pass through the earth. In many ways this is a merciful thing because when judgement finally does come it will be sudden, and terrifying, and there will be no escape.

These tremors of judgement as we get closer to the day have the effect of making as many people as possible look up and consider the days in which they live. It gives all people the maximum opportunity to be saved before it is too late. We are explicitly told God is not slow to fulfil what he has promised, but he is patient because he does not want any to perish, but all to come to repentance and be saved (1 Peter 3:9). This slow wind-up to the end gives all people the maximum opportunity to find God for themselves. Without it people would languish in comfort and luxury, as far as they are able, unaware of the perilous nature of their situation. In many ways we all personally live under this same kind of shadow in any case because no-one knows when their time on this earth is up – their time to die. It is a mercy from God that many do not meet a sudden end because it gives them time to consider their position, and to reach out for God and his mercy. My grandfather was a proud man who would never normally openly acknowledge God, but my mother prayed a great deal for him and on his deathbed he had some kind of angelic visitation that led him to confess what he had seen to us. I know of others that have revived on their deathbed and asked to be shown the way of salvation, then laid back down and died. None of us know the lengths God has gone to in order to save as many as he can. The blood of Jesus is sufficient for all, but not all will receive it. These horsemen are the same mercy of God on a global scale. A way by which men will be inclined to turn to God and be saved while they have the opportunity.

Earlier I said that the troubles and tribulations of our day are part of this last day's tribulation. Does that mean that the horsemen are already released? I believe there is a timeless element to it, as there often is with the things of God – such as the statement that the Lamb has been slain from the foundation of the world (Rev 13:8), even though we only see it actually happen much later in the age – and that he (God) chose us in him from before the creation of the world (Eph 1:4), even though we come to God in our day and our time. Similarly I believe there is an aspect of these horsemen, or a foreshadowing of them, that is happening now, but there is a fuller 'end-of-the-end-times' manifestation of it still to come. I likened the present troubles to be like the normal troubles of a pregnancy, but they are set to be totally eclipsed by the full manifestation of at the end when the actual birth pains come.

FORESHADOWING
Foreshadowing is something we see throughout scripture where events point to something greater coming in the future. Consider Abraham going to sacrifice Isaac on Mount Moriah – which was probably Calvary, the very place of the future cross of Christ. It foreshadowed the greater thing that would happen 2000 years later, so it was a prophetic act.

Jesus referred to Noah being saved from the flood and compared that to the time of the end – so many see the ark being lifted above the judgement as a foreshadow of the rapture (Matt 24:37-39).

In the same way events like the two world wars may well be a modern day foreshadowing, especially if it was an attempt of Satan to extend his kingdom to earth before his time, as I suggested, which is what will happen in a bigger way at the end when he is finally forced down, but will then lose his place in heaven at the same time. The end result of WW2 was to bring a time of relative peace, and to re-establish the nation of Israel, which I am quite certain was not part of the enemy's plan.

These foreshadows are very real in their day, but they also point to a greater thing that will be fully manifest later towards the end of the age. Quite possibly the events of the decade following 70 AD were actually a foreshadowing and not the final fulfilment – even though some of it was clearly direct fulfilment of the words of Jesus.

Similarly when Jewish people try to make sense of Isaiah's prophecies about the coming of the Messiah – Born of a virgin, Prince of Peace, Mighty God, Emmanuel etc. and his sufferings – they make an argument that Hezekiah was the fulfilment. A weak argument, I know, but there were things about it that made them think that, but it was no more than another foreshadowing of the coming of Jesus. For those that thought the foreshadow was the final fulfilment, it would have made them miss the greater event it pointed to, as it still does.

The sacrifices of the Old Testament themselves foreshadowed what would happen to the Son of God in later times. Foreshadowing is yet another form of prophecy from God of what is to yet come that God frequently uses. We therefore see both the horsemen released now as a foreshadow, and we wait for their full release towards the end of the era of tribulation, before the day of wrath.

Compare the following scriptures...

Matt 24: 24b ... *Jerusalem will be trampled on by the Gentiles until the times of the Gentiles are fulfilled.*

Rom 11:25-26 ... *I do not want you to be unaware of this mystery: A partial hardening has come to Israel until the full number of the Gentiles has come in, and in this way all Israel will be saved. As it is written: "The deliverer will come from Zion; he will turn godlessness away from Jacob. And this is my covenant with them when I take away their sins."*

What we know is the gentiles have trampled on Jerusalem since 70 AD when the Romans destroyed the city, but that came to an end in 1948 AD when Israel was rebirthed as a nation, although the gentiles could still be considered to be trampling it in view of the Muslim Mosque, *The Dome of the Rock*, that remains on the temple mount. Today the new state of Israel has jurisdiction over the whole nation, including Jerusalem, but the Palestinian Muslims that occupy parts of Jerusalem have control of the temple mount. I happened to try to visit the Dome of the Rock at the wrong time and I was turned back at gunpoint by their guards. I have also been with the orthodox Jews and seen them wailing at the Wailing Wall and the tunnels beneath. It is the wall that separates the Jewish quarter of the city from the temple area that they don't possess. What are they wailing about? – Everything, but particularly for the return of that part of the city to them on the other side of the wall which they see as a sacred place. These are people that don't even know or accept the words of Jesus or Paul about the times of the gentiles. The return of Israel as a nation is a highly significant event, but it represents only the beginning of something. At present Israel is still truly hardened as the majority of it is atheist as a result of the holocaust, though minorities of all religions are there. When we see Israel suddenly realise Jesus was and is their Messiah and they begin to turn to him, we know then the times of the gentiles are at an end and the time of Christ's return is 'right at the door' (Matt 24:30-33).

When we look at Old Testament scriptures there are clearly many places where we see 'manifold meaning'. Sometimes they seem to skip from verse to verse from one time to another, as if they are overlaid. Take for instance the main scriptures describing Satan as the guardian cherub before he fell. These scripture were really written about the nations around Israel in the day they were written, but they also clearly have this higher heavenly meaning (Ez 28:13-19). Often in the writings of the Old Testament prophets there are things that point to their own day and time, but they also point to coming events. All of this is foreshadowing – another form of prophecy. A very strong example of that is the exile of Israel to Babylon in 587 BC, and the prophecies of their return. That return was made in the time of Nehemiah, but this whole thing also foreshadows the later and greater events of Israel's being scattered to the nations following 70 AD, and their recent return in the present day in 1948. Those prophesies had manifold meaning so the events of Daniel's and Nehemiah's day were themselves a prophecy of the return of Israel towards the time of the end.

When we look at the events Jesus foretold there is clearly this very same kind of manifold meaning in his words. He spoke directly about the destruction of Jerusalem by the Romans in 70 AD, but his words also had a higher meaning that pertains to the time of the end of the age. Those events in Israel are estimated by Josephus to have resulted in 1.1 million killed in the nation of Israel and about 97,000 taken as slaves, at a time when there were 40,000 people in Jerusalem. Consider that now there are more than 7000 times as many people on earth as those killed in that fulfilment and there we see a relatively small event in history used to foreshadow massive events at the end of the age that will involve the whole world. If it only refers to 70 AD then the global context of some of the words of Jesus would seem exaggerated, but it is the fact that his words also point to the end of the age that makes these prophecies fulfil their global scale, rather than just applying to a small occupied country of the Roman Empire.

When Jesus spoke of the sacrilegious object that causes desolation standing in the holy place (Matt 24:15) he spoke both of the Romans invading the temple, and at the same time of the appearance of the antichrist at the end that this foreshadows. He could have used either the words 'Romans', or 'antichrist', but instead he chose descriptive words to cover both meanings. When Jesus told them to flee to the hills it was both an instruction to escape the Romans, which the Christians at the time did, but it also speaks of rapture at the end where the people of God will be caught away. That is why Jesus specifically used the word 'flight' to describe that escape (Matt 24:16 & 20). Every word Jesus spoke is loaded with manifold meaning.

The events of even earlier times that foreshadowed both the destruction of Israel in the time of the Romans, and the destruction at the end of the age in the time of wrath, is that of the judgement of Sodom and Gomorrah. In that instance the 'flight' of Lot and his daughters foreshadows both the flight of the Christians from the Romans in 70 AD, and the rapture that will come at the end to escape wrath, so there we see at least three events linked by foreshadowing. What happened to Lots wife as she looked back foreshadows those that will be left behind in the day of wrath to face judgement because their hearts love this world, and at the same time it applies to those that tried to save their possessions in 70 AD and were caught by the Romans. John told us directly – Do not love the world or anything in the world. If anyone loves the world the love of the Father is not in them (1 John 2:15).

When Jesus spoke of one taken and another left when the son of man returns he spoke of the rapture, but no doubt it also had application to 70 AD (Matt 24:40). The warning to us is that we must remain ready for it (Matt 24:42-44), which we certainly cannot be if we believe it was all fulfilled by a foreshadow and therefore not relevant to us, which is a belief some hold today known as *Preterism*.

Let's sum up this phenomenon of foreshadowing. It is a remarkable phenomenon of the Bible that shows it to be written by a mind greater than ours. When it comes to the coming end-time judgement those foreshadows are comprehensive, as we would expect them to be for such a key time. Let's reiterate:

1. The great flood with the escape of righteous Noah and his family above it as it was used to judge the earth.

2. The judgement of Sodom and Gomorrah with the escape of righteous Lot and his daughters.

3. The judgement of Israel in 70 AD and the escape of the Christians who are made righteous by the blood of

Jesus and who heeded the warning of Jesus to flee and not look back to this world.

Together these are three significant judgement events of the Bible all foreshadowing the end, showing the same elements of the righteous escaping the judgement as they will through the rapture at the end.

Some argue – but doesn't God love the people of the world? Would he really judge them and destroy them?

- First let me answer that the Bible carries the warning that it is coming and virtually all people know about it, especially in our information age. Jesus spoke of it in three of the four gospels – Matthew (24), Luke (21) and Mark (13). The fourth gospel writer, John, wrote the whole Book of Revelation and warned of the antichrist in his letters. Peter wrote of judgement in his letters. Paul wrote of the ends times and the antichrist. Isaiah wrote of the judgement of the world in the Old Testament. Daniel clearly wrote of it in scripture that clearly show they are accurate prophecies by the way events have unfolded in the world. But there are many more warnings in the scriptures also giving the same message either through foreshadow, an image, or a direct message.

- Secondly in my response to whether God will judge the world; look at the judgement that Jesus, the Lamb of God bore on our behalf. The nature of it reflects the gravity of the situation and the fact that judgement of all fallen beings MUST happen.

- Thirdly I answer that God will do everything possible to bring salvation to the people of the world in the end times, and that is the reason for the horsemen of the apocalypse and the end-time tribulation. It is necessary for God to shake the world to save as many as possible before judgement comes, and as such it is a holy act of love and righteousness on the part of God. Through it we can expect to see an incredible end-times harvest that will require all hands on deck when it comes so we should pray to the Lord of the harvest for the workers needed, as Jesus suggested (Matt 9:38, Luke 10:2).

- Fourthly this is not just a judgement of men but of the principalities and powers that caused the evil in the first place. For them there is no escape. For men there is a way out but they must want it, and voluntarily take it or they will be caught up in that judgement. What we know is a great multitude too great to count will make it. Such a number requires the kind of population we see in our day so this again points to it as an end-time judgement and not something small scale from the past.

The HORSEMEN of the APOCALYPSE
Coming back to the earlier point, when we look at the two scriptures I referred to earlier (Zech 6 & Rev 6) we see the same coloured horses (note: the dappled horse and the green horse are correlated as a dappled horse does often have a pale green appearance). Here is a very interesting thing we get from combining these scriptures – All of the horses are sent to go throughout the whole earth but three of the four horses are given a direction of the compass in which they set off once they are released.

BLACK Horses – NORTH
WHITE Horses – WEST
GREEN/DAPPLED Horses – SOUTH

RED Horses – No specific direction given

To understand these directions we must of course know the starting point – where these horses go out from. There is an easy and obvious answer to that – Israel. Israel is the focus of the whole of the scriptures so that should naturally be taken as our reference point. In many ways Israel sits at the centre of the earth, where the continents meet. Looking at the map it is a kind of geometrical centre of the main land mass that includes most of Europe, Africa, and Asia. All of the horses are told by the Lord to go throughout the earth so we can infer from this that the work of each of these horses applies to all the earth. However the directions suggest there is some special application of the particular horse to their given direction, and especially for the black horse as we are told it '*finds rest in the land of the north*' which is the direction it travels. This implies for the black horse there is some kind of exclusive application to that direction. Having centred on Israel we can now compare the Rev 6 prophecies for each of the horses with the direction they set out.

WHITE Horse – the work of this horse is to unleash forces that go out to conquer the earth. They release the restraint on evil forces of conquest and we are told this horse travels west. West from Israel takes us into Europe and North Africa. The remarkable thing about this is that these are exactly the regions where the world's greatest conquests have occurred, and have spread from there throughout the world. Even more remarkably all this began with the very next empire after this was written in the time of the Persian Empire in the Middle East. Alexander the Great was from Macedonia and Greece in Europe. First he overthrew the Persian Empire, and then spread from there to much of the known world, so the centre of conquest became Europe for the first time. From there we see all the major conquests of history occurring and spreading throughout the earth – Roman, Ottoman, Spanish, Portuguese, French, Dutch, German and British, with the British Empire finally covering a quarter of the globe and a third of the people. North Africa was also frequently part of the area of conquest including the Romans, the Crusades, the Ottoman, Napoleonic, British, and both the two World Wars – the greatest conquests ever known on earth. From Europe conquest went across the globe to India and China, and to the America's and Australasia. All of this shows a stunning fulfilment of the Zech 6 and Rev 6 prophecies combined for the white horse. Remarkably the direction for this horse was prophesied when empires were focused on the Middle East, not Europe, and there was no reason to expect such a shift – the beginning of that with Alexander the Great was almost miraculous given the odds against them succeeding as they did against what appeared to be a far superior foe.

GREEN/DAPPLED Horse – Rev 6 tells us the green/dappled horse is named *Death* and his companion *the Grave*. In fact all the horses involve death but each has its different form and means to cause it. In this case it is by the sword, famine, disease and wild animals. Then looking at Zech 6 for the direction of the green horse we are told it heads south. Again starting from Israel south emphatically points to Africa. Once again this horse goes throughout the earth so we expect these things to spread over the whole earth, but this specific direction has a strong correlation to what is prophesied. In Africa we instantly recognise it to be a main place for famine and disease, and even more so for death by wild animals. In that respect Africa seems to be by far the most dangerous place with its huge populations of animals like lions, crocodiles, snakes, hippos and others. Also it is a place of constant conflict between tribes where people are killed by the sword. Of course the sword is only symbolic rather than literal so even guns come into that bracket, but in Africa we see many cases of cruelty and slaughter, more than the rest of the world in such events like the genocide of Rwanda. In truth all these things happen all over Africa and only seem to cease at all for short periods in local places before flaring up again. Compared to other parts of the world it is a rare thing for African countries to have a peaceful and stable society that are not prone to break down into violence again. When we think of plagues, Africa is the place most identified with those events. Even modern plagues such as HIV/AIDS and Ebola seem to have stemmed from there. Generally the climate, the flies/mosquitos and the lack of water make the spread of disease a constant problem. We are also told this horse of the apocalypse is given authority over one fourth of the earth. Africa is in that ball park as a proportion of the earth, though some parts of Africa are always at peace some of the time. Generally when I look around the whole globe at the conflict and disasters going on it does seem to me to be in this kind of proportion most of the time – a fourth of the earth. We are certainly never free of it so it is always an ongoing phenomenon.

BLACK Horse – In Rev 6 the black horse seems to be given authority to make the staple diet of food scarce, though the luxury goods are available and unaffected. Zech 6 suggests this horse focuses on the north, which would be Russia, and that this form of tribulation/trouble would be more exclusive to those parts. This is probably harder to assess in history. No doubt there has always been scarcity in Russia due to its climate that reaches the extremes of both extreme cold and heat. Someone noted you never seem to see Russian restaurants in the west, and they suggested it was because Russia was never really rich enough to develop such cuisine. They were more concerned with survival in the face of shortage. Russia does always import grain and relies heavily on other countries to supply its staple diet. In our day Russia is highly dependent on oil for its income and wealth. When the oil prices dropped in recent years Russia's financial reserves were quickly drained to the point that their leaders started investing their last reserves in agriculture as a last resort to feed the people due to fears of possible starvation and the possible loss of funds to afford outside support. Fortunately the oil prices rose again but it showed how vulnerable they are to these shortages. This reference in Rev 6 to not damaging the oil may well refer to that as their source of wealth and the thing they depend on so completely. Certainly oil may be seen as more of luxury product as it relates to cars and vehicles whereas their real need is for basic staple diet food. Notably those countries that have oil are rich through it, so it is a real source of luxury, though Russia generally needs it merely to subsist, which seems to fit the prophecy very well.

RED Horse – In the case of the red horse we have a kind of opposite case to the black horse which was localised to one direction only as it came to rest in the north. The red horse by contrast has no specific direction and truly goes throughout the earth so its effect applies everywhere. This horse specialised in taking peace from the earth so evil forces are unleashed that lead people to kill and slaughter each other. For this horse the symbol is a mighty sword. We already had a sword with the green horse in Africa but that was only part of the means of death for the people there. Here we have a mighty sword suggesting slaughter at the hands of man on another and much larger scale. Some would ask how this differs from the white horse. The answer is the focus of the white horse is conquest – the building of empires – but this is simply conflict between people and it is something that happens from time to time all over the globe. It includes battles for territory, battles over racism and genocide, battles over resources, and simply murder, where people are simply in a state of hatred and conflict with each other. Battles between drug barons qualify for this kind of trouble, and so do territorial battles on the streets of cities as we see in some countries where law enforcement has broken down.

Beyond the four horsemen in the first four seals there is of course the fifth seal that is all about martyrdom of believers. Again we have seen this happening in many places since the church was born and it will continue to the end, as Jesus warned directly, probably with increasing intensity towards the end. I mentioned before that God's timeclock on the end is in fact the number of martyrs that have come in (Rev 6:9-10). At the moment we see more than 100,000+ martyrs per year, and sometimes many more.

This leads us up to the 6th seal which is special in that it is a winding up of the age of tribulation ready for the transition to the day of wrath. I have already written write extensively about that.

All said, these prophecies together give us a remarkable correlation with what we see and know of in the world, both in history and in our current day. The horses are already unleashed, but there is probably yet to be a much greater fulfilment in the final years of the time of tribulation when the final birth pains begin. As I said before, there is a timelessness in many prophecies so it doesn't necessarily mean these trouble are going to come only at one time and in a strict order. In the Zech 6 scripture the horses are in fact all released together rather than sequentially as it may appear in Rev 6. Also when it states the directions of the horses in Zech 6 they are given in a different order to Rev 6 so it is unlikely that there is a specific order to it. The horsemen of the apocalypse have been released, they operate together in different places in some cases and they have more influence than others at different times. They will see different and increasing levels of fulfilment as we approach the end of the time of tribulation to where there is a birth – a rapture – and the day of wrath begins on earth.

If examining these scriptures does nothing else for you, it should make you realise there is some real and true correlation here to what has happened since we were given these prophecies, and to what is happening right now. We know for a fact these words were given long before most of the fulfilments we can now see. This should serve to alert us to the reality of the scriptures as a whole and make us sit up and take notice of what it says. The book of Revelation gives a stern warning to anyone that seeks to alter it in any way (Rev 22:18-19) but it begins with the promise of blessing to the one that hears and receives it (Rev 1:3). What I have found is these things have the effect of sharpening our spiritual senses so we understand our purpose and God's plan. All I can do is add my voice to that message, for what it's worth. We must heed the things God has shown us and not shy away from them just because they seem hard to face. Every promise God made to help us and keep us stands true to the end, just as much as the words of the Book of Revelation. When we read these things we should always remind ourselves of that immutable fact. In truth these things will not harm you, they will bless you. Yes God MUST wind up this age because evil cannot continue indefinitely, but he has done everything necessary to bring you home to something far better than this world. Right now we live in the trenches of warfare. We need to ask him to give us a real vision and desire for those the things of heaven beyond instead of us clinging to the flimsy earthly securities of this evil world. Then as the scripture says, we will *look up for our redemption is drawing near*. What we hold back by our presence here on earth and our authority will be withdrawn with us when the end of the tribulation comes. Why would we want to be here for the season of judgement that follows? God has plans beyond it that we will be part of, and we may well play a vital part from a higher position even while God judges the earth. Remember we are his children, and you are his child. There is no way he will ever pour out his wrath on you because he is a good parent – a great Father, and he is doing what has to be done, and doing it not just well, but to perfection. So trust him!

9. The Victory of the Church

So far we have focused on the gathering storm of the apocalypse, but I did introduce the 100 year prophecy by Bob Jones that I believe is the other perspective of this from the point of view of the victory of the Church and the Kingdom of God in the last days. Let's take a closer look at that.

In many ways both a large part of the Church, and the world have been sleeping. In fact in giving us an image of the end times Jesus gave us the parable of the wise and foolish virgins that were suddenly awakened when the call went out that the bridegroom had arrived. Interestingly even the wise virgin were caught napping and had to wake up and trim their lamps. We are also given a view into the probable state of the church in the last of the letters to the churches in Revelation, which was to the church of Laodicea. They were described as lukewarm, miserable, poor, blind and naked, having locked Jesus out of the church. They were advised to open the door to him again and get from him the things they needed to rise out of their pitiful condition. What we know from the parable is some will wake up and refocus, while others will suddenly realise they are simply not prepared.

At the same time there are parts of the Church in our day that are fully engaged in the battle. These are people who are engaged in prayer and intercession, and who are using the power of the Spirit God has given us to undo the works of the enemy and keep him at bay. The world is really unaware of how much of this is happening that benefits them and allows them to live a peaceful life, but things are set to change. As a result of this work of the church Satan is restrained from doing what he wants in this world while we are here. For those who are sleeping they are living on the benefit of those who are battling, but the battle is set to heat up and more forces of the Church are needed to wake up and become active – to engage in the battle and in the work of the harvest that will come in the last days of the tribulation.

To highlight the kind of battle that some are currently fighting for God's Kingdom on earth to keep Satan at bay, take a look at the videos linked below in the further reading. This shows that some are fully aware of the battle and they are engaged in it, otherwise things on earth would be a whole lot worse than they are (Russ Dizdar).

The situation for Satan in this time of tribulation is that he is not the ruling power but he is restrained. Earth is the domain of the Church that has been given authority to rule. Satan's forces are therefore operating like a guerrilla force trying constantly to get a real foothold, but so far he has been prevented from doing so in any major way. After the rapture this situation will change as Satan is permitted to become the ruling power for a short time, and the people that turn to God in those days will be more like the guerrilla force. However even then God will be helping them in various ways so they too will still be victorious in the day of wrath even though there will be suffering and many losses, and in this way God will again display his keeping power.

But what about what will happen before that day of transition from tribulation to wrath. We already said the horsemen will be releasing more scope for Satan to create trouble/tribulation in the world, but at the same time the Church will be emerging into the fullness of who and what it takes to combat these forces. God has given us an insight to that through Bob Jones's 100 year prophecy, of which the last 40 years are yet to be fulfilled.

In this time we are going to see all the things Bob spoke of happening in the Church. That means we are going to first come into incredible REST in order to face those increased troubles. What will become stark and obvious to the world is the incredible rest of the people of God while the world becomes more and more fearful of the events it sees taking place in the world. Many will come to Christ because of it.

Next we will see the FAMILY of God released in a way that means we come to support and defend each other in ways never known before. Again this is very much a response to the troubles of these times where the Church raises a powerful shield of protection. Again many of the people of the world will see it and come seeking that protection as the times become increasingly troubled.

Next we see the KINGDOM of God will be discovered in a new way. That means the power of God to counter the advances of the enemy will emerge, proving the people of God to be in control of the earth, even in the face of the formidable forces unleashed in the last days. Again people of the world will realise they need that power and protection and therefore they will come looking for God.

Finally the SONS of God are revealed where the fullness of who and what we are is made manifest in the earth. This is in fact what Paul tells us the whole creation is waiting and groaning for. It is the very purpose of the age. God is displaying his power over evil through his people to its fullest extent. No days like it have been seen before. Both the power of evil will be given more scope to operate in the world as the tribulation progresses, at the same time as the true power of God will be released to match it in the true Church. Those people that refuse to come to God in such times only prove they are making a deliberate and determined choice not to follow God and so they can have no complaints when they come to face the day of wrath.

All of this amounts to a display of last days victory, so it is not a time where the embattled church simply needs to be rescued, and this is the way it will be right up to the end when the Church is snatched away – victory. While they are here on earth they will be holding back the tide of evil. Only when they are gone will that tide truly come in when the Antichrist is free and able to take form in the earth for a while.

The message to us in all of this is IT IS TIME TO WAKE UP! We need to lay aside our preoccupation with comfort, as if we are here to stay. We need a better vision of heaven. If we really had that then we would feel like the apostle Paul did – that we are ever ready to go, but just staying here while God has a job for us to do.

In difficult times I once got a glimpse of the New Jerusalem, which is heaven, and literally felt the comfort of that place. It was only a glimpse but it was enough to change my outlook for life. Everything here is temporary and will pass away. We have a greater cause. Ask God to reveal enough of that to you to get you out of any malaise you may feel you are in right now. Mediocrity as a believer is really not a happy place. We are powerful beings designed to be on the offensive against evil and only when we are achieving that is life really fulfilling. Searching for that fulfilment in other places is futile – especially places offered by the world. Don't just live for a better house or a better car, as if that will finally fulfil you. Take out that sword of the Spirit and instead of living on the defensive trying to protect your comfort zone, get into the battle to make the enemy submit and give the people of this world a taste of the Kingdom inside of you. In any case when the tribulation in the world starts to increase you will find you will be forced into a choice on these things, as many already are when they face persecution and possible martyrdom. You are a son of God, and that means you have a job to do.

10. Summing Up Prophecy

Let's now take a final look at some of the many interpretations and ideas of end-times prophecy that are out there and see how it aligns with this.

There are more than a few who have come up with a whole scheme on what all the end times prophecies mean. For myself I did make a kind of disclaimer that says only part of it is revealed and that God will unfold more of the full meaning when the time comes. That said my message here is that the times may be approaching so it may well be ready for a much fuller understanding. There are certainly many things in the world that seem to be lining up now. For the scheme I am offering here I haven't necessarily covered all the details, but rather gone for the main message and the overview, and focused more on the things that come next that will affect us most rather than delving deeply into the things that come later and that may not actually affect us directly – i.e. the things of God's wrath or judgement on earth. There is always a level of mystery to these things, which is something that I am personally glad about. The wait-and-see aspect of it all is really exciting, and can be scary if you have any doubts about God's keeping power whatever happens.

So to look at other ideas and schemes: There are those who have a whole scheme that is what I and others call 'triumphalist' meaning they see the world as constantly improving and it will continue to do so until God fills the whole earth and evil is driven out. Among them are some who believe they will be part of a generation that will not die, and in fact Bob Jones did say more or less this in his prophetic word that I focused on – though maybe the real fulfilment of that is that some will be raptured. For some of those who hold this view they don't reject the apocalyptic scriptures but see them as fulfilled already back in the decade from 70 AD. We already discussed the idea that though what happened in 70 AD was clearly a direct fulfilment of the words of Jesus, yet there are some much greater things prophesied and they pertain to the time of the end, or the events of that time are a foreshadow of the end as we have seen in so many other cases.

I certainly don't react to these suggestion like some do on these things which is to jump up and down shouting heresy because it is not the orthodox view, or even close to it. End times study does demand an open mind to some degree, and that kind of reaction doesn't help. What I must do though is point out the stakes involved in getting this wrong. Those who believe in difficult times to come will of course be prepared for it in some measure, whereas those with triumphalist views are going to get quite a shock if they are wrong and they may find it hard to face for that reason. What is clear is that these views are so far apart they are mutually exclusive – they can't both be right, unless those events are seen simply as a foreshadow rather than the fulfilment. For that reason it is best we make our minds up about it and get some fairly certain convictions. For myself the main thing I follow in my spiritual life is personal revelation and I feel much of what I am bringing here is exactly that, as I already explained. A good portion of it came to me in a season in 1985, some of it around 2010, and some of it is very current pointing to events in 2020, which is my main reason for writing. Of course my revelations must prove to match the scriptures but what I am saying is my primary source is direct – the same source the scriptures themselves came from.

I have friends who believe in the triumphalist view and the fact they hold those views doesn't alter the fact of our friendship. In fact when seeking God about all this he actually dissuaded me from trying to convince them otherwise, telling me they could not be convinced. That doesn't mean they have it right, of course, so how are we to resolve this. My answer, I believe, is that I am led to point to the events of 2020 and let them speak for themselves. When that comes it may be a message to them, to me, or to us both. In truth if I am wrong about all this then for me that is a pleasant surprise because things may be much easier than I thought, but the reality is at this moment I don't believe their views are correct. I find my personal revelations, as I have shared them, and the message of the scriptures overwhelming. I do see tough times ahead, so I want to be prepared, and I want as many people to be aware of it as possible so we and our faith are not shaken when it comes.

One thing about my interpretation of prophecy I explained in terms of Cinderella's glass slipper; when things come together they just fit. You don't have to shoehorn history or your ideas into them. If you are forcing it then that is a sign something is wrong. I find triumphalist ideas give me that forced sense on many aspects of their interpretation of scripture. That leads me to suspect there is some fear driving it – a way to find security in an insecure world. For myself my way in life has always been to face things directly rather than try to avoid it, but I realise we don't all operate like that. For some false security is better than no security – at least they feel able to get on with their lives that way. In my view not facing things is not the way I live because when it does finally bite you it is going to be so much worse. On the other hand if we do face up to the truth, even if it is hard, then there is an adjustment that goes on with God's help where you learn to live with it, and then even rise above it. After all, every one of God's promises to us stands whatever happens so we have every reason to remain rock steady as we face the truth and place our feet on the Rock.

That is all I can say about the triumphalist view – it is a case of wait and see. For the other views that do believe in end-times troubles let me make some alignments with them – not the details but the main ideas of these schemes. The interesting thing about this is that many of them seem to me to have an element of truth, though I believe it is often is some way lacking or misapplied.

Before we leave that triumphalist idea let me say that the final outcome of the age in the apocalyptic idea is an astonishingly good one, just as the triumphalist believe, but it only comes after passing through the necessary time of wrath, or judgement. God has promised us that when we finally see the outcome of it all it will be greater than anything we can even think or imagine.

PRE-TRIBULATION – The idea that the rapture comes before the tribulation. The answer I have given is that the rapture comes before wrath, but not before tribulation because tribulation is simply trouble, which is even happening now, though it may be big trouble towards the point of transition. Jesus told us in the world we will have trouble, so that is guaranteed. Pre-wrath rapture would be the correct idea. In this case the pre-tribulation idea is based on a wrong understanding of tribulation that includes the time of wrath.

POST-TRIBULATION – The idea the rapture comes after the tribulation. This is correct but only if you understand the term tribulation correctly and don't include in it the time of wrath as some do. The transition takes place on the breaking of the 6th seal.

EARTHLY HOPE/HEAVENLY HOPE – These ideas are held strongly by the Jehovah's Witnesses, but also by others including the triumphalist to some extent. They believe some have a heavenly destiny, and others an earthly destiny. I believe this is true in the sense that only some belong to the body and Bride of Christ, and they will be raptured before wrath is poured out – i.e. they will be gathered when Christ returns. Others will miss that window having failed to be ready for his return, as Jesus told us to be, and find themselves forced to go through the terrible time of wrath where God's judgement will be poured out on earth. These people will either by martyred and die (and maybe join the bride) or come through and survive that time to occupy the earth in the millennium and beyond, so their path into eternity will be different. Eventually the spiritual entity of the New Jerusalem, which is heaven and the abode of Christ and his Bride, will come down and be set on earth, so the natural physical world and the spiritual world become very close. Will the path of those that come through on earth eventually converge with the true Church – I don't know. It may finally converge, or God may have different plans for these two groups – one more heavenly based, and the other more earthly based. As I said, I don't know. We are told when it comes the great mystery will be revealed so I guess there is something there we are not intended to know now. My feeling is that some have pushed their schemes into the unknown in order to complete it and made some blundering errors by doing that.

When it comes to who will be part of the great multitude, who are the Bride of Christ that are raptured – I have a broader view of that than many do. The reason is first of all the scripture tells us they are from EVERY language, tribe, people and nation. I take that literally. I believe God has a people there who are a complete record of the age and able to bear a full testimony to the whole of it. Jesus told us that for us to see heaven we must be 'born again' – which in the original language means 'born again from above'. It is a spiritual rebirth; a heavenly rebirth. Some consider this experience of born again to have begun when Jesus said it as it was a new teaching, or when he died on the cross, but if you look closely at his words in John 3 you see he indicated it was true long before – he just revealed it to become an open truth whereas before it was more of a secret that each one simply discovered personally for him/herself. If this were not true how could Jesus rebuke Nicodemus for not knowing this truth as a teacher of Israel (John 3:10)? All men have had the opportunity to find their way be born again and have their heart changed by God's leading to it. When Jesus came he brought something new, which was to be filled with the Spirit and with power, but born again is something that applied to David, Daniel, Job etc. – Job said '*in the end my redeemer lives and will stand upon the earth*' even though he didn't know the actual name of the one who was to come. When the scriptures tell us we are all saved by the name of Jesus, that doesn't mean everyone knows the name by which they are saved, as those before Christ came didn't. I believe I have met born again believers in all walks of life. Sometimes their religious ideas are very different to mine but their hearts bear evidence of that born again transformation. I was once led to go to Jerusalem and there on the streets of the city I spoke to an old orthodox Jew who explained to me in his broken English that what matters is a changed heart. I heartily agreed, and I believe he had it. It is the church that has tried to narrow that one down to those of their party, and sometimes that even means just their denomination or church. But that is just another case of man getting in the way of God's truth for his own benefit. That harvest will be a great multitude, too great to be counted, that come from all times, places and walks of life in this world, and their gathering is the event of the age. All of them come in by finding their way to faith in God's grace.

PRETERISM – The idea that the apocalyptic scriptures have already been fulfilled in 70 AD. I already covered this in several places earlier and explained that 70 AD was fulfilment, but it was a foreshadowing of the end, as it was for other judgements recorded in the scriptures. To find these arguments search this document for the word 'foreshadow'.

Finally, I would advise any that are thinking of following a course that is focused on this world to lift their sights higher or they may miss the very best and find themselves facing the very opposite scenario.

11. Final Thoughts

In time, after the last days of this age and beyond the millennium era on earth, after Satan is loosed again for a short time and the people who formerly failed are proven to stand fast in the face of his renewed attempts to corrupt them, then the New Jerusalem – Heaven will come down to earth so all of God's people in heaven and on earth will together move into a whole new era that God has planned for us from the beginning of time, and that is beyond anything that any of us have ever thought or imagined. The whole of this first age of man will have served its purpose of securing eternity from ever facing another fall. We the people of God with our testimony of this age will be part of that guarantee. It was always God's plan in the event of a fall to eliminate the possibility once and for all time, which is why the events of this age will have been so epic. They will stand as a record of what evil is, and what it does in its rebellion from God. This age has also served to reveal God in ways far beyond anything that was possible without the fall. In the same way that we look back on Israel and its history, to learn from it, and other parts of history like the world wars for example, so these events together with the events of the last days will complete that horrific record ensuring there will never be a repeat of the fall. That, combined with the Lamb who was slain living with us through the ages of ages to come, bearing on his body the marks and record of the cost of redemption, is everything that is needed to make us secure so God can trust us with eternity, with power, and with perfect freedom. God is an awesome parent and every creature will in the end see that all he has done was necessary, and he has done all things well.

This text has focused on the events of the End Times, but in these last comments I allude back to another book I wrote some years ago called *God's Plan for the Ages*. This book takes a deep look at the bigger picture of God's plan and purposes here on earth in this age, so that may be of real benefit for those of you that want to explore it. For me it was a most fulfilling exploration of God and his plan that forever changed me in the writing of it, so I can't help myself but recommend it as a way to really broaden your mind on God's eternal purposes for us.

TREVOR MADDISON

APPENDIX 1

This is the appendix I mentioned in the preface that I added for the benefit of those that have little no experience of prophecy, and for those that have no faith in these things. If that is you then let me first welcome you. I am about to explain some things that may have escaped your life experience until this point, so I am hoping you will realise that this book is no work of fiction but is in fact based in realities that are firmer than anything you have yet encountered.

Prophecy, which is what you are about to encounter in this book, is what we Christians call a gift of the Spirit – meaning a gift from the Spirit of God, which simply means it is from God. This gift does not stand alone but it is one of a number of gifts that God gives to his people that are in constant use by many Christian believers out there who have discovered them. In fact the real gift that many have discovered is that of the indwelling of the Spirit of God himself by whom these things come, and the fact that he can fill our whole being with his presence, if we let him. Those who have discovered this truth are living a whole new kind of life. You may never have heard it put this way before but that is the truth of what is going on under the radar in the lives of many people. One thing the Bible says is that 'the sons of God are led by the Spirit of God' (Read Romans chapter 8 in the Bible). People who have the Holy Spirit within them really are living a different kind of life – something Jesus called an *'abundant life'* or *'life in all of its fullness'*, and in fact to become a *son* as this describes does in fact depend of whether we have that experience of God.

At this point I hear two main questions coming up from many of you as you read this. One is – *How do I get this experience?* – and the other is – *Is this really real?* Let me answer this last question first as that clearly needs to be resolved before you can contemplate the other. As I said earlier, prophecy is just one gift of the Spirit. Another is healing, and another is miracles. In about 2006 I began an adventure with these gifts on the streets of various cities in the UK. I already believed in them because I had read and believed what it said about it in the Bible, but this was where I actually began to do it in a significant way. It began with me watching short leg bones lengthen and broken bones heal almost instantly as somebody prayed for them in the name of Jesus. In fact the first such healing or miracle I saw myself through my own prayers was of knuckles regrow into the fingers of a man who had an accident with a circular saw seven years earlier and he had severed his forefinger and middle finger but the surgeons had stitched them back on. The knuckles were destroyed so the fingers we useless, but during prayer for his healing I watched his fingers first change from white to red as his blood flow was restored, and then the knuckles grew back into his finger and he began to bend them, which would have been impossible because his guiders had been severed. In truth one of his fingers remained stiff even though it had straightened and blood flow was restored, but that is the kind of mystery we learned we sometimes encounter, which is something I won't get into here. My point is, this is another gift of the Spirit which in this case is pretty convincing as it involves actual physical bone growth, and since then I have seen all manner of physical conditions healed, often instantly. Healings and miracles of this kind have been verified by doctors, and nowadays there are many examples of it actually filmed and released on YouTube. Is the gift of healing real? – I offer you an emphatic yes and I can't think of what better evidence to offer you of this that solid bone growth. In the same way prophecy is also just as real. In fact the Bible suggests it is the greatest of the gifts, even above healing and miracles. If you need more proof than my word on this then you have to dig it out for yourself. The experience is there to be had if you look for it. As many Christians know prophecy does not always foretell the future as some think. In fact prophecy can be simply defined as God speaking through his people. Often it simply takes the form of encouragement, which should not be surprising because God is an amazing parent who cares for us with everything we need to live and thrive. Sometimes, however, prophecy does point the way to the future, and this is certainly the case in many of the Bible prophecies, but it also happens frequently in the use of the gift among believers who have God's Spirit within them.

That brings us back to the prophecy I am offering you in this book. Again the Bible is full of instances of this gift. In fact the book in the Bible I will be going to most is wholly prophetic – the one that appears last in our Bible – the Book of Revelation, written by the Apostle John who personally saw and lived with Jesus during his ministry, and also wrote one of the gospels in the Bible about his experience. That doesn't mean that we have fully understood this book. Much of its language is symbolic and needs interpretation. Not all prophecy is like this, but in these cases there is a level of mystery to it that requires us to engage with God to get answers about its meaning, which is precisely what I have done in the prophecy I am giving you, and I have been 'led' by God to write about it and release it so what you will read is a God given prophecy, given for a right time – now, and not just something of my own creation.

Now, that brings me back to the first question I believe many of you will be asking – *How do I get this experience of God's Spirit within?* Do you have to become 'religious'?

– No. Do you have to begin to live a good life? - No. In fact this last idea is more of an impossibility for you than you may realise because the real problem we all have is more of the heart than the behaviour. Those things we do that show we are beings with a real problem stem from the heart so it is the heart that must be changed for real goodness to begin to emerge – and this is true for every one of us. Outward behaviour does not solve that problem. It has to be dealt with within, and that is not something you can do for yourself – it requires another miracle, but one that many experience every single day in our age. In short the reality is God must do it, but he will only do that when you invite it because he doesn't simply muscle in on our lives and force himself upon us without our consent. He gave you sovereign free will over your own life so you get to decide what happens with it. Therefore this must be a choice that you make for it to happen. Is God willing to do it for you? Emphatically YES! In truth he is longing for you to make that kind of surrender. He loves you. You are his creature. But like all others you are broken and need to be fixed. As the one who made you he knows how to do it and he has put everything in place, which was quite a costly thing I might add. If you look at what Jesus suffered on the cross to make it possible you will realise that is the measure of just how much God does love you and just how far he is prepared to go to restore you to what he made you to be. God has done his part, but now you must do yours, and it is done by turning to God and inviting him to come in – though one thing I must add – this must be a wholehearted decision for you. It must be a decision to give your whole life to him so you too can be led by the Spirit of God. For me, as one who has been living that life for more than 40 years now I can tell you it is an exciting thing – life in all its fullness. But it is also at times extremely challenging because God goes to work on us to transform us completely – how we think, how we live, what we love, what we enjoy, what we do. As I said, he is your maker and he knows what you were made for. All that will be recovered if you choose to walk this path, but you must be ready to leave your old life behind because this one will be entirely new. Those old problems you have may not instantly disappear, but you must set yourself against the things you know are wrong. That is what we call repentance, and it is an important choice to make. God is the one that is committed to do that work in you and it will be a lifelong experience where he works on one thing after another, with the promise of eternal life hereafter. For me I wouldn't have it any other way. His ideas are always so much better than mine. The greatest part of this is that what you will enter into is not 'religion', but a personal relationship with God, and that is the most valuable thing in the world. Like an unbreakable marriage he promises never to leave you or forsake you, and with God he never breaks his promises.

You may need a little time to think this over, but if you decide to go ahead then what you need to do is simply but sincerely pray a prayer like this, and mean what it says. If you are ready to do that then this is all it takes. Here goes:

Dear God, I realise I have been living my own life until now, but now I want to surrender my life to you so I can live the life you are offering me. I here and now turn away from all that I know is wrong and ask you to forgive me for my sin. Thank you for what Jesus did for me on the cross. Please come into my heart today. I give my life to you. Please give me your Holy Spirit and come and live in me. Make me your child today, right now I ask. Thank you for your promise to save me. I now commit my life to you. Amen.

What do you need to do now? Just start to enjoy your new life. Let him lead you. Ask him to show you the way. He will lead you to the people and the things that will help you grow in your faith. Remember, this is a relationship, a personal one, and God wants you to enjoy his company every day, so speak to him, and listen for his response. If you fail in old ways then realise God is on your case to change you – just keep turning back to him. That path of change is the smoothest when we stay close to God, as many of us have discovered. But what you have now is personal to you, and your relationship to God will be as unique as you are, so enjoy it. You are now a child of God.

Further Reading & Resources

The YouTube video of Bob Jones and his 100 year prophecy from 1950's to 2050's
https://www.youtube.com/watch?v=qZJzwnyLod0

The following link is by a man called Ken Peters who some decades ago had a very impacting vision of the world in the time of wrath. I find this has nothing that disagrees with the events I have been describing and I feel it is an authentic prophetic revelation so I want to highlight it and recommend it. As scary as it is it gives a vivid view of what it would actually mean to be left behind.
https://z3news.com/w/ken-peters-tribulation/

The following links are the message of a man called Russ Dizdar as an example of the work some parts of the Church are doing to restrain the satanic forces on earth using their God given authority.
Part-1
https://www.youtube.com/watch?v=ozDnBzDEWjo
Part 2:
https://www.youtube.com/watch?v=5kuhpsDvDZ0
Part 3:
https://www.youtube.com/watch?v=leW609DcppY

To better understand some of the comments in this book on God's big plan in creating this world, including his reason for allowing evil for a time in this age, the following book may offer some answers and give you some valuable insights into the truths of God and his plan. *God's Plan for the Ages by Trevor Maddison.*

NOTE: This book – The 2020 vision of the End Times – is not for profit. I have released it either free, or through some channels as cheap as I can make it with no profit to myself. There is therefore no financial motive in it for me. It is simply an important message I believe I am commissioned to release at this time and it is therefore my service to you. You are authorised to distribute it freely at no cost in its unaltered state. May God lead you in doing that.

Trevor Maddison

47188677R00065

Printed in Poland
by Amazon Fulfillment
Poland Sp. z o.o., Wrocław